Pour Angélique

Proving the True Story of Oak Island

Mars Stirhaven

First published 31 October 2018.
Flowing and Print-Replica ebook versions are available.

Published in the United States by Mars Stirhaven, Payson, AZ.
Library of Congress Control Number: 2018913096
ISBN 978-0-578-40346-5

First Edition

8 9 10

For the Angels

WOM[GWQSN[IJMILFVHLWUTNMWLWV
UFWJSQNYIVYSF[QO\HOR[NS'MYE]
HQNTJXXTWJLMBTHWNHQUNS^JMSTL
[/LPKYJFXNPTVJRHPTCRHKSXIRFV
GAPDTQKKYUXUMZTNTAYQTHMFTLXX
HTKH;20@BTLUZNOFPWFTERRVPQYC
UXUV\QPZHRZOM]P]OUC[IObKILXE
JFEB_ULL^IMYNWK]NERRZPVOTCIO
K]UWPMVIHXIMM[T[MVNBXKPLTPFQ
WVMQJATEGNJVRXEOJJVLSVKIOVPK
HHLO^UIR]EXPPKR]WO[YWJTZ3.55

Pour Angélique

Contents

L'introduction

In the 18th century a minimum salary of £40 a year was required to support a family and to live a comfortable life £100 a year was needed.

—The Royal Mint[12]

On September 11, 1746, the Money Pit was filling up with water and loose soil. A few days later, *La Grande Société* would succeed in pulling off the greatest heist in history and begin the biggest cover-up ever. The £2,000,000 buried on Oak Island would have been worth 20,000 years of comfort. It would have been worth billions, maybe even a trillion, today.

Part I

Angels and Mathematicians

Chapter 1

Les Ange ℓs

[This chapter intentionally left blank.]

Chapter 2

Le Mathématicien

Passwords, Enigmas, and Pirates:
Search for Irony

September 11, 2018

The Mathematician sits down at his home computer, ready to begin typing. Next to the stack of papers on his desk is a Double Gulp from 7-Eleven. The operating system prompts him to upgrade to *Bionic Beaver*. He fumbles a few times typing his password. He tries a few combinations before he gets it right. He knows the password. *I know the password. Is that the password?*

His wife is out; the kids are watching TV. He knows his time is borrowed. His wife would be making a brief appearance soon. His youngest daughter should be in bed. He amuses himself with the parallels of this and that of Angélique. He clicks to open his favorite search engine.

define irony. He scrolls past the first entry that doesn't seem fitting. The second entry reads:

> Irony | Definition of Irony by Merriam-Webster.
> the use of words to express something other than
> ... the literal meaning.[5]

Angélique is not his daughter's name, but it is French. Well, to him, her name is a term used in mathematics and a compromise on the spelling. He notes the impending subtlety here, too, especially in the spelling of names. He brings up a calculator and types

$$2018 - 1746$$

Should Sallaberry's little Angel be elsewhere, at this very moment, 272 years earlier?

He clicks on the *Bionic Beaver* upgrade to proceed. He amuses himself with the name of the upgrade. He also feels a slight frustration waiting for the installation to finish. He knows that he doesn't have to wait, but he does.

He realizes that he hasn't been on the computer much lately. *But still, the coincidences in the name and timing of the latest operating system upgrade are amusing.* He has spent the summer in the United Kingdom, visiting Bletchley Park and the castles of *Northumberland.*

He immediately finds even more patterns and relationships here, with the names and nature of the places he visited and how they relate to his current undertaking. He pushes these thoughts out of his mind as he brings up his text editor. He pauses to decide if he should encode the letters of his favorite text editor in the text. But then he realizes that he still hasn't determined the significance of the letters "vi" that were found on that bit of parchment paper by the early Oak Island treasure-seekers in the bottom of the Money Pit. He contemplates the significance of the letters for another moment. *I hope it isn't this. If it is, it's probably useless!* He smiles at this and then pushes this thought out of his mind.

He types two titles and leaves the first chapter as an exercise for the reader. In truth, at this very moment in time, he still doesn't fully understand the significance of the two angels. He types the month and the day. *September 11.* He pauses, thinking of the significance here. Too many relationships come to mind. His mind floods and fills with thoughts. He pushes them out.

He asks his favorite search engine for the date of the attack on the two towers. The search returns *2001*. He remembers what he was doing but not the year. He second guesses himself on typing the current year. 2018. *Yes, I think that's right. I don't recall seeing 2019 yet.* He has always been bad with dates and time.

He's also bad at arithmetic, but he knows that you might have already guessed that from his use of a calculator to subtract 1746 from 2018. He removes two lines of text, then undoes the removal. He amuses himself with this and the parallel to time travel. He thinks of Einstein and relativity. *Only traveling forward in time is possible, not backward.* He smiles to himself, thinks briefly of Oak Island time travel conspiracies and then pushes these thoughts out of his mind. *They don't... lead... anywhere...* He becomes distracted. *Searching for irony and only finding 2.71828182845904...*

He decides to leave the references to arithmetic. His time is borrowed. He pushes this out of his mind and then it floods right back in. Despite being bad at arithmetic, dates, and time, he's actually a well-respected mathematician.

He's published a number of papers and he's proud of his Erdős number.[2] He keeps his manuscripts with his most prized possessions. In any event, he thinks to himself: *Mathematics has provided for his family and to his family.* He notes deep relationships here.

He suddenly realizes that he must be less recursive, to make more progress in less time. He inserts a reference to his identity. He pauses and then wonders about the true identity of *Le Lionceau de Talmont*, the Lion cub of Talmont, the cryptic signature found on Zena Halpern's Oak Island map[3].

September 22, 2008

The Mathematician is at the Wild Animal Park in San Diego. There are two lion cubs, nearly adult in size and much larger than the Mathematician. Despite their size, the lion cubs are still playful. The cubs try to get the attention of their parents. One of the cubs gives up and lies down on the ledge of the enclosure next to the glass. The other cub catches the stare of the Mathematician. The Mathematician thinks back to a game he used to play with his calico cat, Euler.

The Mathematician hides behind a post and stealthily stares at the cub. The lion cub also seems to enjoy the game and stealthily does the same. *If the glass disappeared, what would the lion cub do? Would the cub just want to play?*

---

[2]think degrees of separation from Kevin Bacon, but for mathematicians

[3]Zena Halpern was a contemporary author and Oak Island researcher

The lion cub charges at the glass and pounces, swiping at the Mathematician but only contacts the glass. The Mathematician is startled at first, but then finds security behind the thick glass. *Is this game going to make it harder on the zookeepers?*

The Mathematician and lion cub play this game for a few minutes, each appearing and pouncing at the other until a crowd gathers and begins taping the event with their cell phones. As the Mathematician leaves, the lion cub is still trying to attack the gathering onlookers through the glass.

The Mathematician's thoughts begin to fade to the present. He notices he's staring into the glass of his computer monitor typing a story about lions. He thinks of Ray Bradbury's "The Veldt" and how he is a lion cub in a virtual reality. The Mathematician searches: *distance to Talmont. Only 3,758 miles for the Mathematician to become the Lionceau de Talmont! I'll have to take more time off work.*

September 11, 2018

The Mathematician realizes that he has been taking a lot of time off work, more than usual. He's also been sick for the last few days, recovering from a cold. He corrects a typo, spelling code instead of code. His mind pauses at an infinity. He suddenly knocks off a stack of papers from his desk and manages to reset his train of thought.

Part II

La Grande Société

Chapter 3

Le Contrôleur

Beavers, Indians, Governors?
Or Talmont?

September 11, 1739

The Comptroller[1] sits down at his desk and begins rearranging a stack of papers that had recently fallen into disarray. A large inkwell and a nearly empty glass of wine are on his desk. The lamplight flickers as he struggles to read a letter. The letter is not addressed to him but he reads it as if it were.

> *It will be addressed to me in the future; the dispatches from Maurepas will soon be for me! Who has Maurepas's ear? I have Maurepas's ear! Soon, I will even have the ear of the ....*

At this moment, the Comptroller leans closer to the desk, brings the letter to a 45 degree angle with the lamplight, and

---

[1] a controller of finances

15

shifts more of his weight from his chair to the desk. The shift causes the uneven legs of the desk to tilt.

The Comptroller, distracted by this, repeatedly presses down on the desk and releases, causing the desk to tilt back and forth. *The desk is in need of repairs.* The Comptroller begins scrutinizing more of his surroundings. *In fact, everything is in need of repairs.* He would see to them at first light.

Just two days earlier, the Comptroller arrived with the newly appointed governor, Isaac-Louis de Forant, aboard the vessel *Jason* captained by M. de Vaudreuil. The Comptroller, also newly appointed, is eager to impress the Grand Conspirator, the mastermind behind *La Grande Société*.

The Comptroller was to relieve Sieur Sabatier and Monsieur Boucher who were increasingly needed elsewhere. Within days of his arrival, the Comptroller sets about learning everything he can about Île Royale.

The Hiriards own most of the port. They own half of the harbor and two-thirds of the other half. The patriarch of the family is now Sieur Jean Hiriard. The Hiriards spend most of their time elsewhere: Bordeaux, Talmont, St. Jean de Luz. Their presence is still felt in their absence. In fact, fishermen like to stay on the Hiriards' good side. They pay the Hiriards for the use of fishing grounds they don't even own.

Jean Hiriard has the well-weathered look of a sailor but is dressed like a French colonial officer of the court. His mind is sharp and he has a strong physique.

Aye? My age? Ayes, the years have only slowed me. We be owin' my good condition to the want of drink and temptation; allowin' for the proper

*amount of restraint and indulgence before my just
damnation.*

Jean is a cod fisherman of sorts. He's really a captain, a merchant, a shipowner of many vessels of varying size and state of repair. The corruption of the port affords him opportunities in smuggling: tobacco, sugar, slaves. He doesn't see himself as a smuggler.

*Ayes, a smuggler be a merchant who's caught up
in the enterprise of the moment, havin' evidence
enough to warrant a conviction. Bein' neither
caught, nor in possession, I be but the merchant.*

Hiriard, once a master unto himself, has now come to see himself as the humble servant of more than one master. Despite the wealth of merchants and the landholdings of a lord, Hiriard considers himself at the mercy of his unseen masters. The Comptroller knows that something continues to hang over Hiriard's head. Even so, Hiriard manages to bury these thoughts deeply and hides them well.

At the age of 74, Hiriard, being almost twice the age of the Comptroller, still has a style and confidence of a man-about-town. The Comptroller thinks of being back in Talmont, his days of prowling about and playing the gallant. The Comptroller still likes to think of himself as *Le Lionceau de Talmont*.

Hiriard is well traveled and knowledgeable. While the Comptroller prides himself in the courses he's taken and the books in his possession, Jean's wisdom comes from his travels and apprenticeships.

Hiriard speaks many languages with varying degrees of proficiency. He speaks with an accent that is hard for the

Comptroller to place. *Cornish? Basque?* He extends his *r*'s and labors dropping his *h*'s.

Hiriard has assimilated into the role of patriarch through his age and association, through his marine career where he's helped build the colony. If he were married, the Comptroller thought to himself, it would have only been a formal arrangement.

Hiriard has served his country in some capacity since the summer of 1702, but still feels indebted. The Comptroller feels as if he's known the Hiriards for years. In fact, the Comptroller has known the Hiriards for years, but the Comptroller knows that he can never reveal this association.

███████████████████

The Comptroller.

Chapter 4

Le Capitaine

Michel de Sallaberry was a smuggler. There was no doubt about it.

Circumstances didn't afford Sallaberry an easier life and he knew it. He wanted more. He wanted a larger vessel. He wanted the command. He wanted recognition for achievement. He saw smuggling as a necessary evil to succeed in the port. The smugglers had larger vessels, bigger contracts, and better payouts.

Sallaberry wanted to see himself as a sailor, a father, a ship's captain. Sallaberry would keep his descent into corruption secret while his family enjoyed the ascent.

Sallaberry would die November 27, 1768, taking his secrets to the grave. Born on the 4th of July, 1704, he would, without ever knowing it, have a lot to do with America's independence 72 years later, to the very day.

Michel was the son of Marsans de Sallaberry and Marie de Michelance, born near Bayonne. Michel followed his father to Quebec in 1733. In 1735, he was identified as a captain. While the Hiriard captains were sailing under false surnames, Michel began his career using his real name. The Hiriards had a network of notaries: connections that could provide passports, identification, and all manner of documentation. If the Hiriards needed certificates of birth, baptism, or marriage, they knew how to obtain them.

The Hiriards sailed routinely between France and Canada and the West Indies. They always signed at ports using their real first name—the name their crew would attest to—but always a fake, often new, surname.

Surnames seemed to be more flexible in the 18th century; they indicated a place of birth or a landholding or an occupation and could be ditted to mean many things, like Pierre de Reynier dit Regnac, for example.

Spelling errors also seemed prevalent. Many people were unable to write and names were often spelled phonetically by someone else. In France, with a number of silent letters, this gave a great deal of leeway in the spelling of names. In New France, this would be compounded by a plethora of accents from the melting pot of colonials.

First names, on the other hand, had very little variation; they were taken from the French Calender of Saints with few exceptions. Hyphenated names could be attached to the first name to give a more unique sounding name and middle names could also indicate parents, etc.

Sailing under fake names was not new to Jean Hiriard, he had been doing it for nearly his whole life.

During the 1740s, the Hiriards were either incredibly unlucky or exceptionally bold. After the Comptroller arrives in the colony, the Hiriards' shipments were almost always found to be damaged, captured, or run aground. The Hiriards wouldn't sail unless their shipments were insured. The Hiriards would end up making significant claims on almost all of their vessels and goods. The Hiriards, of course, were really perfecting the art of smuggling and insurance scams.

In 1736, Sallaberry procured a small 68-ton brigantine, renamed it after himself, *Saint-Michel*, and started carrying cargo between Île Royale and Quebec. He would soon find better opportunities amid all the smuggling and corruption in the colony. In 1741, he was shipping the same cargo to the same destinations as the Hiriards: Martinico, Saint-Domingue, La Rochelle, Bordeaux. He would become well associated with the Comptroller and the Hiriards. Around this time, *La Grande Société* employed Sallaberry and Hiriard to dispatch secret messages between the Comptroller and the Grand Conspirator, and to other, even more confidential, locations. By 1745, Sallaberry was well trusted and was working very closely with the other conspirators in carrying out their ultimate conspiracy: *Le Grand Plan*.

On May 17, 1735, Michel de Sallaberry married Marie-Catherine Rouer de Villeray. She would die five years later leaving him with only a daughter, Angélique. In 1746, Angélique would have been around the same age as the Mathematician's daughter. Doubtless, Sallaberry would refer to his daughter as the Mathematician did his: his little angel, *mon petit ange*.

The Mathematician wonders if Angélique sailed with Sallaberry during these years. *Was little Angélique there on the Island of the Two Angels near Newfoundland or was she being looked after by someone else?*

Sallaberry didn't remarry until July 30, 1750. Madeleine-

Louise Juchereau Duchesnay de Saint-Denis. They would have a son, Ignace Michel Louis Antoine Sallaberry, on July 5, 1752. Ignace's descendants would eventually ignore their patriarch's spelling of Sallaberry and seek a claim to nobility as d'Irumberry de Salaberry.

The Mathematician wonders if Sallaberry would have considered himself *Le Lionceau de Talmont*, being the protégé of Jean Hiriard, the real lion of Talmont, the fierce conspirator with blood already on his hands. Of course, despite Hiriard being a real lion, Hiriard on his deathbed would draw himself as a lion cub, *Le Lionceau de Talmont*, looking hopelessly across a pond, longing to be with his Swan.

Sallaberry ended up retiring from the Navy and living out his dying days with his daughter, Angélique. The Mathematician was sure that Sallaberry would tell Angélique the stories of his past:

> *Hundreds of iron-bound chests packed floor to ceiling. Each filled with treasure. The sound those riches made as I picked them up and dropped them back into the chest. The sound they made as I ran my hands through them.*

Stories so fantastic that Angélique wouldn't believe them. Stories the Mathematician didn't even believe. As Sallaberry would sail past Mahone Bay, from Halifax to Port Royal, he would point off into the distance and tell Angélique:

> *There! Off the islands over there. Those are the islands named after you. L'ange. Below that is where we buried the treasure.*

The Oak Island story will remember Sallaberry as the captain of the schooner *La Marie*.[104, 77]

```
Michel de Sallaberry,
The Captain.
```

Chapter 5

Le Sculpteur

Voila Le Vazeur

Pierre-Noël Levasseur, Jr., was the son of a master sculptor and carpenter. The Levasseurs descended from a long line of master carpenters. Levasseur's father wanted to pass on the family trade to his four sons. He also wanted help running his business in his aging years.

Levasseur's father was also trained in sculpting by a master sculptor of Quebec or Montreal. Levasseur's father would have also wanted to pass this expertise onto his children.

During the early 18th century, sculpting and carpentry were trades in high demand in New France[1]. The colonies were developing quickly and many new churches and parishes were being constructed. Gilded furniture, oaken cabinetry, and sculptures of all mediums were needed for the new places of worship.

---

[1]explored parts of North America, Nova Scotia, and Newfoundland minus British holdings

$$\beta \quad \Sigma \quad \Delta \quad \Theta \quad X_T P \quad \zeta(2)$$

On May 31, 1737, thanks to his "talent and experience," Levasseur's father obtained a commission as royal surveyor and geometrician in the government of Quebec.[42] The Mathematician is certain, by his own experience, that the father would have also wanted to pass this knowledge onto his children.

The Mathematician has learned very little about Levasseur, the son of the master sculptor. The Mathematician's searches have discovered much about the father, but not much about the son. One of his internet searches resulted in the following information about the father:

> One of the most beautiful ensembles of sculpted wood that exists in the province of Québec is found at the Ursuline chapel. The objects were created by Pierre-Noël Levasseur between 1723 and 1739 and were transferred to the present-day chapel.... The objects were gilded by the Ursulines themselves. L'ange à la trompette and the retable, the two being important pieces of the décor, bring out the exceptional richness of the chapel.[14]

The Mathematician is taken aback by the ornate golden gilding of the father's masterpiece and imagines how the son would have been impressed by the father's work.

The Mathematician eventually stumbles upon a contemporary newsletter commemorating "the sons of the sculpture Pierre-Noël Levasseur." The Mathematician learns that the father gave up trying to train one of his other sons and sent him to study with a fellow cabinetmaker.

Monsieur,

Thank you for accepting my son as an apprentice. I hope he appreciates learning the trade with you and I agree with the conditions outlined in your letter.

I will be paying you thirty pounds per year, and I appreciate that you will be like a father to him. I am confident that you will be giving him some time to write, read and to draw. If he needs paper, I will send some.

I ask that you keep a watchful eye on him as if he were your own son. See to it that he goes to Church, receives the sacraments and avoids places of drunkenness and debauchery.

I pray that you will be taking my place as a father. Let him know that I must punish him for all the sorrows he has caused me and my wife and that he leaves me at a time when I could use his services.

He never would listen to me or his mother's advice. I hope God will give him the grace to be more sensible in the future.

Do not let him know how much I still care for him but make him realize the hurt he has caused us.

— Pierre-Noël I[57]

The father is said to have focused his training efforts on his three other sons, although the training for Pierre-Noël II, born October 25, 1719, had been inexplicably cut short:

The colony required specialists for the ornamentation of the King's ships built in Quebec. Pierre-Noël II was sent to France to learn and improve his skills as a sculptor of ornaments for ships. In the Fall of 1743 he boarded Le Rubis to the arsenal of Rochefort for a stage as an apprentice. He returned to New France in 1746 and after a short stay, for unknown mysterious reasons, he went back to France. Pierre-Noël II pursued his career in Rochefort until 1763 and then signed a contract with the Chamber of Commerce of La Rochelle to sculpt ornaments to decorate the buildings of the Stock exchange. Completed between 1763 and 1769 these sculptures of maritime inspiration are still in place and remain a testimony of his skills as a sculptor. Though he left no traces, Pierre-Noël II Levasseur never came back to his country of origin.[57]

The Mathematician is intrigued by the mystery surrounding Levasseur's trip to Quebec in 1746 and the traces he was careful not to leave. He finds a longer article in French. He translates it using his favorite search engine. He copies and pastes small segments into the translation service,[3] which only accepts 5,000 characters at a time, and then pastes the results back into his text editor. The translation is rough, but the Mathematician finds it both necessary and sufficient.

A Levasseur at Rochefort

Jean BELISLE

The year 1984, like everyone knows it, marks the 450th anniversary of the official discovery of

CHAPTER 5. *LE SCULPTEUR*

Canada by Jacques Cartier.

On this occasion, Canada and Quebec, in particular, revive the maritime traditions that have shaped them. The sail returns to the fashion...

...

In the autumn of 1743, Pierre-Noël's son embarks on Le Rubis for Rochefort. He settles there, in January 1744, and begins working there as apprentice sculptor, at the salary of 40 sols per day.[2] A year and a half later, he is returned to New France on Le Fort-Louis. In fact, he was supposed to go on the flute La Gironde in the autumn of 1745, but because of uncontrollable circumstances, he did not leave until the spring of 1746.

His stay in the country must be very short because in the winter 1746, he is back in Rochefort and increased to 50 sols per day. The sculptor's stay in Quebec City is very mysterious because, for a reason that remains unknown, someone contrived to make all traces disappear. In 1788, several people will testify before the notary Descheneaux that Pierre-Noël never returned to Quebec after leaving in 1743. Yet, this stay of a few months is attested in its official record kept at the National Archives in Paris.

What was Levasseur going to do in Quebec? The answer is far from easy.

Logically, he should make sculptures for the king's ships because it is for this kind of work that he had been trained in Rochefort. Expense slips concerning the construction of the corvette Le Carcajou mention a payment of 200 livres to a certain Pierre Levasseur for various works of sculpture. Unfortunately, the date of slip, July 31, 1745, does not correspond to the estimated dates of Pierre-Noël's stay in Quebec City. There may have been a date error, but we cannot assume this. Pierre-Noël's participation in the Carcajou sculpture will, unfortunately,

---

[2]there are 20 sols to a livre, and about 23 livres to a pound of silver (i.e., £1)

remain hypothetical.

In 1748, his salary went up to three livres a day.
During the winter, Levasseur is put in contact
with a Quebec armorer, Antoine Lemaire (whose
activity was between 1748 and 1788), and who was one
of those who testify to the non-return of
Levasseur to Quebec. Essentially at the same time,
the master carpenter Jean Baillairgé (1726-1805)
landed in Quebec and made the knowledge of
Pierre-Noël's father: "The said Sieur Baillargé
said he arrived in this city in the year one
thousand seven hundred forty-eight and that at
times after having made the acquaintance of the late
Pierre Noël Levasseur, sculptor and surveyor of this
City and Marie Agnes Lajoue his wife; and that said
Pierre Noël Levasseur told him then and at several
times, that he had sent his son Pierre Noël Levasseur
to Rochefort and that his son came back two or three
years ago; that he showed him drawings and told him
that they had been sent by his son from Rochefort
where he was to learn and to perfect himself in
sculpture."

. . .

The career of Pierre-Noël Levasseur in France
continued at Rochefort. In 1755, his salary was
increased to three livres five sols a day. Five
years after that, he meets at Rochefort the master
Quebec blacksmith Gabriel Masse, who worked in the
years 1750-1788. The latter, taken prisoner in
1759, in passage to Rochefort en route to Quebec.
According to Masse, Levasseur still works to naval
sculpture: "... that being at Rochefort he knew the
said Pierre Noël Levasseur's son who was working on
sculpture for ships ... "

At that time, Levasseur just left the Navy
Workshop (January 1760), to work on his own.
During the spring of 1763, he gets some kind of
certificate of good services. Curiously, the same
year, September 30, he signs a contract with the
Chamber of Commerce of La Rochelle to run seven
pieces of sculpture to decorate the courtyard of
the Stock Exchange. The certificate may have been
issued to show the people administrators of the
House that Levasseur was free to take the contract
on his own behalf. This is where our original sculptor

will give the best of himself. Payments relating
to the execution of this contract are from October
22nd 1763 to April 3, 1764. The total sum will
reach 1200 livres. The sculptures executed in
1763-1769 by Levasseur are still up on the walls
of the Stock Exchange. The whole is very imposing
and compares favorably with everything that was
made in France at the time. A review at the same
level as the weapons royal, the weapons of the
Marshal Sénectère and those of the intendant Gag.
These coat of arms were unfortunately destroyed
during the French Revolution. Despite the mutilations,
the royal arms executed by Levasseur easily support
the comparison with those that were executed for
the doors of Quebec, about 1750, in antiquity:
compass, nautical chart, quadrant, anchor, trident
of Neptune and others. The importance of this
Levasseur [sculpture is that it] demonstrates,
contrary to the opinions expressed by the steward,
that a colonial sculptor can do as well as a
metropolitan sculptor, if he is well trained. At the
end of his contract in La Rochelle, we lose track of
Pierre-Noël Levasseur. He is then only 45 years old,
and his career certainly continued in France, but for
the moment, the continuation of his history remains
to be discovered.[36]

Pierre-Noël Levasseur, The Sculptor.

Chapter 6

Le Grand Conspirator

Either you are working for your own advantage
or for that of the King. Which do you prefer us to
think?[38]

September 17, 1739

The Comptroller scrutinizes the colonials. He sees some
unable to sign their name, some unable to spell their name.
He watches the ones who claim they can sign their name
struggling to make their mark. The Comptroller's penmanship is perfectly legible, better than Hiriard and Sabatier, but
not nearly as elegant as Boucher's. His own sister is barely
able to make her mark, signing M B.

The Comptroller no longer writes as much as he used to.
He often simply dictates a letter to the Grand Conspirator and
just asks the scribes to read it back, ensuring the exactness of
his expression. He still signs his name with the same rushed
flair: firmly, boldly, and with large letters. The Comptroller
does write to the Grand Conspirator in his own handwriting

but only when he's visiting France, or outside the assistance of his clerks, or when the subject matter demands more secrecy.

The Comptroller's penmanship, like his signature, is also rushed. He acknowledges this. *It's a result of my rare intelligence and the speed at which I need to put thought to paper.* The Comptroller writes with passion. He loves both the laconic and the loquacious.

The Comptroller loves his sister but thinks sadly of her abilities. He acknowledges that her place truly has no aptitude for education. *The social woman is not amenable to education.* The Comptroller also thinks poorly of the colonials and the slaves loaded on his ships.

> *Everyone in Quebec thinks of restoring his fortunes and little of the interests of the king and the colony.*[62] *My only interests are in the interests in which I own a share of the interest.*

The Comptroller would seem intolerant of almost everything and nearly everyone, save a few of his closest associates. Even his closest associates were not unscathed by his scrutiny; he strongly disapproves of Sabatier's lifestyle though he knew better to make mention of it.

To everyone else, the Comptroller fully expressed the tyranny he possessed in his thoughts. In the future, he will come to dictate people's movements and their behavior in every detail. He will prescribe severe punishments for offenders: the stocks, the gibbet, the execution block, the tortures of the boot. As a rare exception to his intolerance, he does come to the defense of the Huguenots:

> *The Huguenot merchants are harmless in religion,*

yet indispensable in trade.[38]

The Comptroller also thinks poorly of the Indian nations. Well, he will think poorly of the savages until a few years later, when he first sees the treasure chamber for himself. The treasure chamber the Mi'kmaq Indians help build. *The Indians in the south* are *hard working.*

In any event, and especially at this moment in time, the Comptroller wants nothing to do with Île Royal. The Comptroller only sees the port as a means to an end. The Comptroller's task is to oversee the financial operations, the commerce, of the port. He knows that he has an even more important mission to fulfill. He also knows that the Grand Conspirator will make him intendant of the French colonies one day.

The Comptroller much preferred, and will continue to request, an appointment in France. The Grand Conspirator told him "an intendancy in the ports of France cannot be expected if one has not served in the colonies."[38] The Comptroller's actions will affirm his belief in this. The Grand Conspirator's actions will betray this promise. In fact, the Grand Conspirator never intended the Comptroller to survive his intendancy.

The disarray of paperwork on the Comptroller's desk was left by his predecessor. The Comptroller loves order. *My attention to detail will impress the Grand Conspirator.* Up until this time, the Comptroller only knew the Grand Conspirator by a different name. Ultimately, the Comptroller would come to know the Grand Conspirator as the mastermind of an even larger conspiracy. *Le grand conspirateur de La Grande Société.*

The Comptroller again sets about reorganizing paperwork. He wants everything to be in its place. *Attention to detail is important.* He learned this in the few courses he took at the Faculté de Droit. He learned it more in his apprenticeship. He would learn it now, in practice, more than ever.

The governor also dislikes his menial appointment to Île Royal. The newly appointed governor doesn't want his appointment any more than the Comptroller wants his. The Grand Conspirator had persuaded them both. The governor would accept the appointment in good grace. The Comptroller would accept the appointment in pursuit of an intendency in France. The Comptroller also aimed at transcending his station and believed that the Grand Conspirator would help him in doing this.

The Comptroller believed his mother was the daughter of a Baron. *How does one verify one's Mother? By paperwork? How does one audit these receipts? Paperwork which can be bought and manipulated, misfiled and lost, forged and dispatched, burned or secreted away?* The Comptroller had a claim of nobility from his mother. From his father, he had seen the advantage having the King's ear provided. His father was Conseilleur du Roi, Counselor to the Parlement at Bordeaux, and Receiver General to the King. His father married nobility; his father only played the part. The Comptroller felt truly noble. His mother was the daughter of a Baron, Commissioner of the Marine, and a representative of an old and powerful family.

Just two months, well 42 days, earlier he had left his home in Talmont. He had left his life prowling at night, the nights of gambling and debauchery. The nights of playing the gallant. Now he would resign himself to the pen, playing the role of the humble servant. A comptroller for now, but always *Le Lionceau de Talmont*: eternally on the prowl, hunger bigger than his appetite; the gambling for stakes as high as at the King's tables; the parties, the pomp, the prestige. The Comptroller dreams of returning to this and even thinks of establishing this in the colony. Of course, the Comptroller also thinks of himself as the real Grand Conspirator of *La Grande Société. You measure strength with me! We will see who proves stronger in the end!*

September 17, 2018

The Mathematician wonders to himself. *Would the Grand Conspirator have known the future Comptroller as resident commissary of the Navy at Rochefort? Would the Grand Conspirator have thought much of the future Comptroller? The Grand Conspirator would have been made aware of the Comptroller's vices. Would you appoint someone with a gambling vice as Comptroller, keeper of your purse-strings? Not unless you saw the advantage, the control, the indebtedness, the eagerness to repay, the lust of want, the plausible deniability that this would provide.*

The Grand Conspirator.

Chapter 7

Le Pirate

My repentance lasted not, as I sail'd, as I sail'd,
  My repentance lasted not, as I sail'd,
My repentance lasted not, my vows I soon forgot,
  Damnation's my just, lot as I sail'd.

The Hiriards are seldom seen in Île Royal. Their interests are managed by others. Actually, the Hiriards do spend a fair amount of time in the colonies. They just spend it under different names. Jean Hiriard, Sr., goes by the name of Antoine Sabatier in Île Royal. Jean Hiriard, Jr., goes by the name of Pierre-Jérôme Boucher. The Hiriards are spies, and those aren't even their real names.

Jean Hiriard Jr's name is really Pierre de Reynier. Jean Hiriard Sr's name is really Robert Culliford. Culliford was a pirate!

The Sabatier identity was created first. In the summer of 1702, Culliford had just brokered his release from Newgate prison and was to become a privateer and informant for the English. Culliford's spymaster, impressed by Culliford's potential, arranged for him to be introduced to an influential

Marquis in France near Toulon.

Culliford's handlers found the recently deceased parents of a Bourgeois family in Toulon: a family without an heir. *Did the Grand Conspirator's father arrange for this family to become recently deceased?*

Robert Culliford became Antoine Sabatier in France, the son Joseph Sabatier and Magdeleine Arnauld never had. The handlers failed to notice that Antoine would have been born 14 years before the Sabatier marriage and that the supposed mother, at the time, would have only been 6 years old.

Sabatier was not Culliford's first alias, and Hiriard would not be his last. Prior to this, Culliford had already sailed under at least two other names and during his lifetime, he would use countless more.

The influential Marquis assisted in establishing Sabatier in the marines as a clerk, arranged for his apprenticeship, and personally saw to his advancement. The Marquis also introduced Culliford to the De Goutins, a family already working with the influential Marquis. The Marquis, the De Goutins, and the English all had different motives, but their interests were all suitably aligned. Culliford, as Sabatier, was to be placed in the colonies to work with the De Goutins. Culliford, as Hiriard, would be heavily involved in the maritime operations and secret communications between Europe and the colonies.

In 1710, the De Goutins and other conspirators aided in the surrender of Port Royal (modern-day Annapolis Royal) to the English. The De Goutins were sent back to France and established themselves in Nantes and Bordeaux, near Talmont. In 1711, Culliford chartered a vessel from Plaisance to engage in privateering off the Bay of Biscay. Culliford, captaining the vessel, took the surname of the cod fishermen of Petit Degras, and the first name of the great consort of his life, whom he had become separated from. He sailed as Jean petit D'Hiriard de Biarritz.

This influential Marquis would also come to claim responsibility for the name: Jean, after his third son; Hiriard, a prominent name already established in the colony.

```
Robert Culliford of Cornwall,
Antoine Sabatier of Île Royal,
Jean Hiriard Sr. of Biarritz,
The Pirate.
```

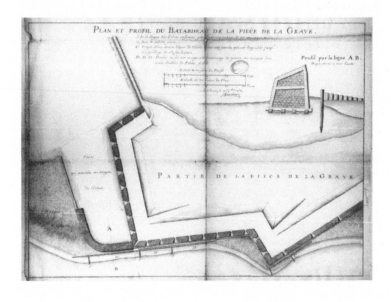

Chapter 8

L'ingénieur

Pierre-Jérôme Boucher, a.k.a.
Pierre Bouchet, a.k.a.
Pierre Bochet, a.k.a.
Pierre de Reynier, a.k.a.
Pierre de Regnac, a.k.a.
Pierre de Barre, a.k.a.
Pierre de Baron, a.k.a.
Pierre Hiriard, a.k.a.
Jean Hiriard Jr., a.k.a.
The Engineer.

The Engineer was a descendant of the Reynier family of the Gironde region in France: the heir apparent to his ancestors' wealth, chateaus and vineyards. A decades long dispute of inheritance had just been settled shortly before Pierre's birth in 1688.

The Reyniers were winemakers in Grézillac near Bordeaux and Talmont. They were the lords of Barre and Bon-

47

net, Baron of Capbreton, and more. The Reyniers leased out their estate in Bordeaux: the Chateaux Bonnet. Owing to the custom of the time, the leaseholders managed the Reynier estate as if it were their own. Culliford and the De Goutins would have called it home.

The De Goutins' visits to Bordeaux between 1690 and 1710, the leasing of the Reynier estate, along with the dealings of Reynier's wine business, and the associations with the neighboring lords of Saint Bonnet, all helped bring the young Pierre into the world of the conspirators. Pierre was born about two years before Mathieu De Goutin's oldest son, François-Marie.

In 1709, the same influential Marquis arranged for Pierre, under the name Pierre-Jérôme Boucher, to begin an apprenticeship in Rochefort. The young and intelligent Pierre would quickly show an aptitude for engineering, drafting, and cartography, providing important capabilities to the conspirators. Pierre would become essential in designing the colonial fortifications and producing detailed intelligence reports for the English.

In 1714, Mathieu, the patriarch of the De Goutin family, died. Pierre and the De Goutins would come to see Culliford as the new patriarch of the family. Culliford would provide the father figure the young conspirators needed. Pierre would continue to grow up alongside the De Goutins with Culliford's fatherly mentoring. In 1729, Pierre would marry Marie Anne De Goutin (Marguerite-Madeleine-Louise Anne), the sister of the Comptroller. Pierre, in the late 1730s, began sailing with Culliford and became a ship's captain on his own. Pierre's son, François, would do the same in the early 1740s.

Pierre remained the owner of the "maison noble de Bonnet" until the winter of 1744, when, in preparation for the greatest heist in history, the young squire, Lord of Barre and Bonnet, former captain of a Normandy regiment, sold the family estate to squire and royal councilor Jean de Chillaud Desfieux, president of the royal court of appeals, for 53,881 French livres.[13]

The Hiriard and Boucher names were already prominent in the colonies and would be welcomed by the tight-knit colonials. The Sabatier, Hiriard, and Boucher names also had the advantage of not being tarnished by the De Goutin corruptions of the past and surrender of Port Royal.

Jean Hiriard and Pierre-Jérôme Boucher were instruments of the conspiracy. They were, in any sense the meaning, creations of the Grande Conspirator and the Grand Conspirator's father, also named Jean and Jérôme. The father of the Grand Conspirator, the influential marquis working with the English, the literal father of *La Grande Société*, was named Jérôme and his third son was Jean.

Jérôme Phélypeaux, Comte de Maurepas et Pontchartrain, Secretary of State for the Marine and the Royal Household. Jérôme's third son, Jean-Frederic Phélypeaux, Comte de Maurepas, was born at nearly the same time Jérôme helped create Jean Hiriard's identity.

From birth, Jérôme raised Jean-Frederic with one purpose. Jean-Frederic was to become Secretary of State to the King of France. Jérôme had purchased the office with a right of inheritance; Jean-Frederic would have *right en survivance* to the position. Jean-Frederic Phélypeaux, Comte de Maurepas, was the Grand Conspirator.[89, 98]

Part III

The Set-up

Capt. Kidd hanging in chains.

Chapter 9

The Real Captain Kidd

Robert Culliford was probably born in Saint Martin on Looe Bay, Cornwall, England as Robert Colliver, March 18, 1665.[21] Culliford might have also signed his last name with a few variations: Culrfoord, Collover, Cullifer, etc. Culliford first met William Kidd as shipmates aboard the French privateer *Sainte Rose* in 1689. They were among the only six Britons aboard the ship. Kidd and Culliford mutinied against the French Captain Jean Fantin. The ship was renamed the *Blessed William* and Kidd was voted captain. William Kidd would turn out to be one of the worst pirates in history.

Kidd was torn by religious beliefs and considered himself an English privateer. He refused to attack vessels that weren't French, at least until his crew threatened desertion or mutiny, marooning or death. The crew also managed to strong-arm Kidd into re-negotiating better shares of the loot. In February 1690, Culliford led his own mutiny and deprived Kidd of his command, stealing the *Blessed William* when Kidd was ashore at Antigua in the West Indies.

Culliford, with Captain Kidd's ship and Captain Kidd's crew, began sailing, whether intentional or not, under the name Robert Kidd, helping William garner a notoriety he didn't deserve, but one that William would pay dearly for.

Culliford sailed around the Caribbean, sacking ships and attacking towns. Culliford amassed a small fortune and securely locked it up in a chest that he kept secreted away. Culliford ransacked and laid waste to two French Canadian towns. Culliford also captured a French frigate *L'Esperance* and renamed it the *Horne Frigate*.

Culliford served as captain, quartermaster, and crew. Seeing the fate of Jean Fantin and William Kidd, Culliford was willing to practice diplomacy and allow others to lead, stepping in to help keep the peace and to provide direction without being, himself, a target of mutiny.

Culliford was known for his fearlessness and had no problems attacking larger and better-armed vessels. Culliford was strong, fair, and honest in keeping to the pirate code. Culliford was very intelligent: he would trick merchants by quickly identifying the probable origin and destination of a ship, running up the colors of a favorable nation's flag on his mast, and lulling the ship into a false sense of security by talking about trade routes and harbors as it approached.

In 1692, Culliford robbed the local population of a village in India. He was captured by Gujarati authorities and imprisoned for four years. In 1696, he managed to escape, commandeer a ship in Madras and return to piracy. Near the Nicobar islands, the crew of the ship he commandeered managed to retake the ship and marooned Culliford on an island. He was rescued by Ralph Stout, captain of the *Mocha*. Culliford soon became captain of the *Mocha*, now bound for

Turkey. He pursued a British ship in a battle that nearly sank both ships. Culliford retreated to Île Sainte-Marie off eastern Madagascar, stealing ships along the way.

While Culliford amassed a small fortune, William Kidd gained very little during his privateering and would turn to pirate hunting. He managed to sell what possessions he had and talk investors into fronting the rest of the funds needed for his expedition. He was fitted out with a new ship, the *Adventure Galley*, ideal for capturing pirates. Once in the Thames, Kidd failed to salute a Navy yacht at Greenwich:

> As the Adventure Galley sailed down the Thames, Kidd unaccountably failed to salute a Navy yacht at Greenwich, as custom dictated. The Navy yacht then fired a shot to make him show respect, and Kidd's crew responded with an astounding display of impudence – by turning and slapping their backsides in [disdain].[116]

The Navy captain retaliated by forcing much of Kidd's crew into compulsory naval service, despite the protests.

Not surprisingly, Kidd also turned out to be a poor pirate hunter. His crew became desperate after Kidd failed to attack many prizes on several occasions. Without the hope of profit from any share of the loot, much of Kidd's crew abandoned him; those who stayed continually made open threats of mutiny. Kidd, also feeling the weight of failure, started to break down.

Kidd is most known for fracturing the skull of a crew member's head with an iron-bound bucket. The crew member was William Moore. Moore urged Kidd to attack a Dutch ship and Kidd refused, calling Moore a "lousy dog." Moore responded, "If I am a lousy dog, you have made me so; you have brought me to ruin and many more."[116] Kidd reacted by snatching up and heaving the bucket toward Moore's head. Moore died the following day. Amidst the constant threats of mutiny, Kidd is also known for having locked himself in the captain's cabin with explosives, threatening to shoot the first person who walked through the door and blow up the entire ship.

On January 30, 1698, Kidd, having no choice, and facing imminent mutiny and utter failure, took a prize at sea: the 400-ton *Quedagh Merchant*, an Indian-Armenian ship sailing under an English captain with passes of French protection. Kidd, realizing the captain was English, tried to persuade his crew to return the ship to its owners. The crew refused claiming it counted as a French ship because it was sailing under French passes. The crew renamed the ship *Adventure Prize* and set sail for Madagascar.

On April 1, 1698, Kidd, having reached Madagascar, finally encountered the first pirate of his expedition: Robert Culliford, the very pirate who mutinied and stole Kidd's ship years earlier. Kidd would likely have ordered his men to seize Culliford and the *Mocha* frigate, but seeing the opportunity to join up with a real pirate, Kidd's crew abandoned Kidd and joined Culliford's crew. In the end, only 13 of the originally intended 150 crew remained with Kidd.

Kidd had his remaining crew set fire to the *Adventure Galley*. Kidd would claim that the *Adventure Galley* had become worm-eaten and leaky. Knowing he was about to face his investors, Kidd might have thought it was easier to return without their ship. Practically speaking, Kidd didn't have the crew necessary to take two ships back and might have thought himself in a position of keeping the ship not owned by the investors. The crew salvaged every last scrap of metal and sailed back to New York on the *Adventure Prize*.

Kidd would soon learn that he was wanted for piracy and that several English men-of-war were looking for him. He ditched the *Adventure Prize* in the Caribbean, sold off his small share of the plunder he managed to keep, hid this small amount of treasure on Gardiners Island, which would later be recovered and used against him as evidence, and continued to New York to face his accusers with his proof of innocence: his Letter of Marque and the French passes. Kidd's investors, fearing self-incrimination and the embarrassment of having sponsored privateering now that the Anglo-French war had just ended, tricked Kidd into giving up his evidence and placed him into custody.

Kidd was sent to Newgate Prison in London to stand trial for murder and piracy. Kidd was stunned by the murder charge. Captains at this time were given much leniency, especially in controlling a mutinous crew. Kidd also considered the death an accident, certainly not premeditated. Kidd was sunk on the coerced, coached and rehearsed, testimony of some of his crew. The same shipmates that would later recant their testimony. Kidd, without being able to manufacture the French passes and Letter of Marque, was convicted and sentenced to death.

On May 23, 1701, Captain Kidd was hanged twice, once successfully, in a public execution at Execution Dock in London. His body was gibbeted and hung over the Thames for three years. The evidence that would have saved William Kidd was intentionally misfiled on behalf of his investors and only resurfaced in the early twentieth century.

Nearly the same time that Kidd was turning himself in to face his accusers, Culliford and his shipmates received letters of pardon from Commodore Warren. Aimed at reducing the pirate population, Warren was offering pardons to pirates as an incentive to give up the life of piracy. Culliford eventually allowed himself to be taken by authorities, planning to display his pardon, settle his affairs, and retire from piracy with the wealth he had amassed.

The pardons were not honored, and Culliford and his shipmates were taken to Newgate prison. Culliford posted bail, purchased new clothing and made himself appear stylish before the trial. Backed by the promise of a large payment from his stashed loot, Culliford hired an outstanding lawyer. Culliford's lawyer convinced the judges to grant Culliford a stay of execution.

Culliford's fellow crew members, also having their pardons rescinded and also turning states evidence, were unable to gain a stay of execution and were hanged at Execution Dock. Culliford's lawyer was able to make the confidence of a leading minister and spymaster in the English government and was able to broker a deal for Culliford's release.

Culliford seeing the direness of his situation, agreed to the conditions of his special pardon. He was to plead guilty and provide testimony to secure the conviction of Samuel Burgess. In exchange for sparing his life, Culliford would serve the English crown as a privateer and informant. Culliford's intelligence; his stylish presentation; his ability to read and write and speak French; his ability to blend in among French privateers; and Kidd, having taken to the grave the notoriety Culliford deserved; all of this and more, impressed the English spymaster and saved Culliford's life.

These events were not at all uncommon. The aforementioned Samuel Burgess, convicted on Culliford's testimony, also managed to secure a pardon for his crimes and signed aboard an English privateer the same year. The Mathematician believes that Culliford would have had a hand in aiding in the release of the man he helped convict. Additionally, Daniel Defoe, the would-be author of Robinson Crusoe, would also be imprisoned in Newgate and would also broker his release in exchange for his services as a spy, just one year later. Defoe's Robinson Crusoe would influence Edgar Allan Poe's "The Gold Bug" and Poe's story would, in turn, influence all of modern cryptography through a young William Friedman[1].[94, 96, 115]

The War of Spanish Succession had just broken out, and the hostilities in the colonies were on the rise. England faced losing their footholds in the Americas to New France. England, after many attempts, was still unable to take over the key ports they desired in the colonies. The English needed an insider, a confidential agent. Culliford, the should-have-been-more-notorious pirate, knew these areas and sailed with French privateers. Posing as a French privateer during the war, Culliford would provide the English with a unique advantage.

The British colonies in America would also learn of Culliford, as Hiriard, an informant for the British in the Acadian Port of Île Royal. Culliford would end up serving the British, the Americans, the French, the Canadians, and the Acadians; splitting his loyalties in a way that only a pirate could.

---

[1]a US Army cryptographer who ran the research division of the Army's Signal Intelligence Service in the 1930s and chief cryptologist for the National Security Agency in the 1950s, making profound and lasting impacts in his field

History remembers Culliford for besting Captain William Kidd on several occasions but then disappearing from all records in the summer of 1702. In truth, the true story of Oak Island will reveal that Culliford bested Kidd once more and that Culliford, as Sabatier and Hiriard, has an even more fantastic story to tell.

Chapter 10

Paule Sabatier

The great consort of Culliford's life is the man that would come to pose as his brother, John Swann (Jon Swan, Paul Swan, etc.).[99]

Swan first used the name Paul when signing aboard a merchant ship, the *Otto Van Tuyl*. Swan had just bought passage to America. Swan had left Culliford twice, in their earlier life together as pirates. When Culliford finally reunited with Swan in the 1720s, Culliford promised Swan an easier life, a life that they could live together, a life that would not put Paul in danger. Swan would play the role of Antoine Sabatier's brother, allowing them the benefit of living together without accusation. Culliford also promised Paul that he would pursue appointments and advancements for Paul in the colony—something Paul would look forward to doing—perhaps the King's writer.

In France, Paul Swan would become François Paule de Sabatier. Swan posing as Antoine Sabatier's brother would also legitimize Swan's right to inheritance if anything were to happen to Culliford. Paule would also marry the youngest De Goutin daughter in what, the Mathematician would believe, was mostly a formal arrangement.

Chapter 11

Pseudo-Bonaventure

```
def pseudo_bonaventure(n):
    """
    a name given to various
    anonymous authors of works
    previously attributed to
    Saint Bonaventure[107]
    """

    pass
```

Bonaventure was said to be the progenitor of the Comptroller. Bonaventure was also said to be a merchant and citizen of Tours. Bonaventure's son, Étienne, would leave Paris around 1619.

Étienne married Marie Renard in 1617. This marriage brought Étienne into the circles of the Bonneaus. Louis was the son of Étienne and Marie.

Louis became associated with one of the most important

tax farms in western France, financed in large part by the Bonneaus, dealing in the imports and exports of Bordeaux. Louis married Anne Fracquet daughter of Denis Fracquet and Renée Bonnet and had a son Louis-Amable.

Louis-Amable married Marguerite Lombard with a dowry of 40,000 livres. The Lombards were part of the local bourgeoisie and specialized in maritime administration.

The Comptroller of our story was said to be the son of Louis-Amable and Marguerite. The Comptroller's name was François Bigot.

Bigot will become a cog in the works of *La Grande Société*: an essential part of the machine which receives motion and engages its teeth to transmit that motion. It is the Comptroller's association with the maritime, with Talmont and Bordeaux, and the house of Bonnet that brought the Bigots, the De Goutins, the Hiriards, Sabatier and Boucher, together. This along with the new plans of the Grand Conspirator who takes over for the Grand Conspirator's father in 1738.

The Comptroller François Bigot would be the Grand Conspirator's greatest creation. He would also be the scapegoat that would serve to protect the conspiracy. The Comptroller's sister would marry the Engineer and, towards the end of his life, Bigot, living in exile, would take one of the many names of his brother-in-law, the Sieur de Barre.

The Mathematician finds several issues with Bigot's genealogy. In short, the Bonaventure source doesn't seem to work.

Chapter 12

Les Portraits

September 30, 2018

The Mathematician searches for portraits of all of the conspirators, something tangible he could display to the reader. The Mathematician easily finds paintings and memoirs of the Grand Conspirator;[26] an engraving that might have been modeled after the Comptroller;[118] an impressive painting of Angélique, the Comptroller's mistress;[118] many pieces of artwork left by the Sculptor;[12, 36] one engraving that represents Culliford and a few illustrations that are inspired by him;[29] several designs and maps left by the Engineer and cartographer;[30, 31] and a silhouette profile of the Captain's son[48] and many paintings, engravings and statues of the Captain's grandson.[53]

The Mathematician begins tracking down textual descriptions of the conspirators. Culliford as Sabatier was always seen as an agreeable man, enjoyable to work with, intelligent and diplomatic. This diplomacy and his ability to keep the peace could clearly be traced all the way back to his days of successfully shoe-horning mutinous crews. Culliford was known to be "daring without a death wish, a man with larcenous plans, a surprisingly good bottle companion; witty, athletic, clearly devious but trustworthy."[119]

The Mathematician was able to find two quotes that help paint the portrait of Culliford as Sabatier and the corruption in the port.

> What can be said about the appearance and atmosphere of Place du Port? The area was occupied from the beginning of the town, and some of its buildings were among Louisbourg's oldest. We may guess that a waterfront square close by the docks and surrounded by warehouses would be less attractive than many other parts of the town, but it should be noted that one of the square's businesses was a ladies' dress shop run by the widow Chevalier. The best comment must be a contemporary one. Demanding the demolition of a number of buildings around Place du Port in 1728, Sabatier, the procureur general, agreed that the irregular alignments and angles of the buildings of the area formed several coupe gorges in which terrible accidents could occur. A coupe gorge is a place where throats get cut. Even allowing for the hyperbole of a prosecutor strengthening his case (for the number of thefts and crimes around Place du Port does not seem unduly large), we can see that the reputation of the area cannot have been high at that time, and the angles and corners of the Place were never entirely eliminated.[15]

The widow Chevalier died on 4 August 1744, in the Rue du Quay house of her son Pierre Belair. At 5:30 p.m., within an hour of her death, procureur du roi Antoine Sabatier visited Michel Hertel de Cournoyer, the acting bailli, and asked that the house be sealed in readiness for an inventory of the widow's property, because one of the principal heirs, a daughter, was living in France and could not be present to defend her interests in the succession. Cournoyer ordered that these procedures begin. Eventually an inventory was made, the daughter was consulted and it was decided that the widow's belongings would be sold.[15]

The Mathematician can trace the same empathy and introspection of Sabatier to Culliford the pirate, when Culliford arranged to have shares of the loot sent home to the deceased members of his crew.

The Comptroller is much the opposite of Sabatier. The Comptroller is overtly ruthless, self-centered and wholly unrepentant. The Comptroller has a youthful zeal and an eagerness to please. The Grand Conspirator saw these as signs of strength and Bigot, overseeing the duties once performed by Sabatier and Boucher, would free up the Hiriards to focus their efforts elsewhere.

Contemporaries of the time left us the physical and moral portrait of Bigot. He was small in size, well made, delicate, but his face was ugly and covered with pimples. He loved gambling, ostentation, and women. He was tall, hard, and difficult for those who displeased him; very judicious in matters that did not run against his own interests, and very laconic in his answers....[118]

Despite the Bonaventure story, the Mathematician has determined that Bigot's origins are shrouded in intrigue. The Mathematician's research into Bigot's genealogy cannot independently validate the Comptroller's origins.[6] His sister is a De Goutin, and his brother is a Ricouart. There is a possibility that the De Goutins are really descendants of Mathieu (Anne Henry) Ricouart.[49] Bigot could have really been one of Mathieu De Goutin's children or the son of a 16-year-old François De Goutin outside of marriage. François De Goutin was married twice, each time to an Angélique.[60] *Were these the two Angels?* It turns out that there were literally hundreds of Angels among the conspirators to account for the Angels the Mathematician was searching for. One was the mistress of the Comptroller, the beauty and tragedy in the Comptroller's life.

> The portrait of Angélique, the sister of Nicolas, presents the beauty in her thirties in Diane, identified by the arrows and the quiver. This Roman goddess comes from the Greek Artemis.

> "Daughter of Zeus and Leto, twin sister of Apollo, born in the island of Delos, she is goddess of the moon (Phoebe, Hecate) and hunting. Equipped with bows and arrows, escorted by nymphs, she haunts the woods at night in pursuit of the big cats. Virgo and chaste, she is vindictive and cruel; it causes Actéon, Orion, Callisto to perish. She helps Apollo avenge the injury made

by Niobe to their mother. Wrathful against Agamemnon, she forces him to sacrifice Iphigenia. On the other hand, she hears Arethuse's prayer, which she transforms into a fountain."[118]

The Mathematician finds it intriguing that Bigot's mistress is portrayed as a goddess, *La Déesse*, pursuing big cats. *Were the Angels of the island named after her?* Was this also the *Déesse* that the Mathematician was looking for? Was Bigot the Lion cub of Talmont that Angélique was targeting with the cupid's arrow? Bigot's coat of arms actually displays the heads of three, big golden cats that look like lion cubs![68]

> Angélique had recently been married to Péan when she became intendant Bigot's mistress after his arrival at Quebec in 1748. Mme Péan had her court, and she made many male hearts shudder. Called "the great Sultane," or "Lélie" for intimates, she had power over the fortunes of her Areopagus, being at the heart of the financial and political schemes of this end of corrupt regime.
>
> "[...] Bigot's system of corruption was purely inherent in a vice-royal court, like the one he established in Quebec City, modeled essentially on the royal court of Versailles: lavish social life, with its happy receptions, its balls and his sumptuous dinners in the midst of a hideously poor population; mistresses, usually the wives of ambitious officers—Michel-Jean-Hugues Péan, assistant-major of Quebec, for example—content

with the continual favors they received in return, and flattered to find themselves in so distinguished a company; promotions, jobs, contracts and opportunities to do business inside these happy circles; a complicated network of loyalties and jealousies among the few favorites, and bitterness among the excluded and the forgotten."

The portrait of Angélique, the work of a very competent painter, was certainly made in France where it is now preserved. But it is quite improbable that it was painted after her definitive departure from Quebec in 1760, at the time when her family was brought to trial in front of the Chatelet. We propose to date it from the glorious period of Madame Péan the huntress, that is during her trip to France with her husband and Bigot in 1754. She was then 32 years old, which corresponds to her apparent age on this portrait which then had to adorn his Quebec residence. The wearing of the head is proud and proud. The arrow, very long and pointed, is held with the left hand, that of the passions. The cherub is about to receive it too with his left hand. The pretty triangular face presents a firm and direct tone where softness and hardness rub shoulders. The look, powerful, penetrating and determined, is wearing a sardonic smirk. The garment of her right breast lifts slightly, and we feel that it will soon be stripped ...[118]

Chapter 13

The French Connection

La Grande Société desired power and wealth; wealth sufficient for gaining power. *La Grande Société* would work closely with the English when it served their interests in France. As time went on and the American colonies continued to separate from the British, the conspirators aligned even more heavily with the Americans.

The connection between Culliford the Pirate and his Swan, Boucher the Engineer, Bigot the Comptroller and soon-to-be intendant, Sallaberry the Captain and smuggler, Levasseur the Sculptor—between the De Goutin, Hiriard and Bigot families—was the Secretary of the State of the Marine: Maurepas, the Grand Conspirator, and his father before him.

The De Goutins were among the first settlers of Acadia (Nova Scotia and part of Atlantic Canada). Though, they were not at all colonists. Their family history documents the fact that they were the construct of an influential marquis. This influential marquis was the Grand Conspirator's father: Jérôme Phélypeaux, comte de Pontchartrain, the Secretary of the State to the Maison du Roi (House of the King) and minister of the French Navy. Jérôme would see to the De Goutin's rise in power. Mathieu De Goutin was born in France around 1663 to a family of the lesser nobility. The earliest references to De Goutin in the Canadian Archives sign the name De Gargas De Goutin. Mathieu might have been from Gargas, France near Toulon and Marseille.

Mathieu is said to have ingratiated himself to the marquis who sent him to Île Royal in 1688 to serve as the King's *lieutenant général civil et criminel.* Mathieu would serve as colonial secretary, counselor, and paymaster treasurer. In 1691 or 1692, Mathieu was granted a seigneurie at Mouscoudabouet (Musquodoboit) in Newfoundland. In 1696, he was granted a second seigneury at Pointe-aux-Chênes, today's Oak Point, on Rivière St. Jean. Around 1689, Mathieu married "foolishly to a peasant's daughter," Jeanne Thibodeau, who was only 17 years old at the time. His marriage, and those of his children, turned out to be prolific. The Mathematician suspects that they might have only appeared prolific. Mathieu and Jeanne had 12 children (6 boys, 6 girls).[10] The oldest son alone, François-Marie, had 11 children (7 boys, 4 girls).[1, 11]

Mathieu was said to be "an undeserving, worthless character, ... (who is) quite stubbornly convinced of his ability, ... (and) sure that the two offices he holds will give him rank and authority here which are, if not above, at least equal to that of the governor." The governor of Île Royal in the early 1700s complained that Mathieu was "hardly in a position to make good judgments [as the colony's chief judge] ... because a third of the settlers are relatives of his wife."[73] Jeanne Thibodeau's parents had 17 children.[17]

The real Hiriards were from the Bay of Biscay in France:

St. Jean de Luz, Biarritz, and Bayonne, not far from Bordeaux. They settled throughout Acadia but especially in Gaspé and Petit Degras. These communities were heavily influenced by the Basques. The Hiriards were sailors and cod fisherman. The later Hiriards were merchants and landowners, importing and exporting cod and cod oil and leasing fishing grounds and the use of harbor areas they owned. The Hiriards and the De Goutins would have become well acquainted as fishing was one of the most important activities in the early colony. A chamber of commerce was founded in Bayonne in 1726, and the cod fishery off the shores of Newfoundland and construction opportunities saw to Bayonne's growth.[16, 92]

Amongst the complaints and growing age of Mathieu, Jérôme began planning for Mathieu's replacement—Sabatier and Boucher. Antoine Sabatier entered the marine service as a clerk in 1703. Mathieu helped surrender Port Royal to the English in 1710. The De Goutins returned to France. In 1714, the Treaty of Utrecht awarded Île Royal and Île St. Jean back to France.[106] Jérôme sent Mathieu back to the colonies and Jérôme would have intended Mathieu to again rise in power to help turn over Île Royal back to the English. Mathieu would, however, die in late 1714. In 1717, Boucher and Sabatier would serve as replacement and come to marry into the De Goutin family. In the case of the Sabatiers, the marriages seemed to be formal arrangements, the wives and children staying in France.

Despite the apparent backstory Bigot's Bonaventure history provides, the Bigot and De Goutin families seem inseparable. The De Goutins, and possibly Maurepas, are Huguenots and hide this to avoid persecution. The Huguenots had been under persecution since 1685 and the persecution, especially after 1715, had only been getting worse. Interestingly, one of the De Goutins is named Abraham. *Abraham, a Jewish De Goutin?* Abraham is also the name of Bigot's and Maurepas's most loyal companion, Abraham Gradis, born around the same time as Abraham De Goutin. The Mathematician suspects that Alexandre De Goutin might have converted to Judaism and taken the name Abraham.

Port Royal had been under mostly French possession and constant English aggression since 1690. The English failed from 1704-1710 to siege the port. The English knew that they needed the Hiriards and their cooperation. They needed the boots on the ground, as the Lagina brothers like to say. The brothers that began unraveling the Oak Island story.

The father of the Grand Conspirator, and the Grand Conspirator himself, struck deals with the English and the Americans, enabling the Minister of the Navy to control the outcomes of the King's expeditions. The conspirators weren't just aiming for the end of Huguenot persecution; they were aiming for something far greater. *La Grande Société* didn't care about France possessing the colonies, they were mostly interested in the story their loss would tell. War, it would turn out, was also a very profitable endeavor, and wealth yields power.

Chapter 14

The Austrian Succession

In the spring of 1744, war officially broke out again between France and Great Britain. Something about the Austrian Succession. Something about something about the Austrian Succession. ....[101, 114]

Part IV

The Hook

Chapter 15

Bletchley Park

September 11, 2018

The Mathematician suddenly knocks a stack of papers off his desk and manages to reset his train of thought.

August 11, 2018

The Mathematician thinks to himself, "A mathematician rides a train to Bletchley Park." He hears an interesting quote that sticks with him. Something about the most significant Polish breakthrough: that it was best to put mathematicians to the task of breaking codes and solving enigmas.

He enjoys Alan Turing's office the most. "Just him and his Chalkboard," he says out loud, "Turing's chalkboard must have been bigger than this! My co-worker's personal, portable, dry-erase board is bigger than this!"

September 11, 2018

The Mathematician writes his co-worker's name but then removes it. He then sees his co-worker's name... More papers fall off his desk. He manages to pick them up, and this resets his train of thought.

Bletchley Park

August 11, 2018

The Mathematician enjoys the pond and the resident swan. He thinks of mathematicians pausing their train of thought and their stay here. He enjoys the adjacent computing museum even more. He finds himself in a quiet correidor, with an old computer. Most of the old computers and code-breaking machines in the museum have signs that ask you not to touch them. This computer is running, has an accessible keyboard, and a prompt he remembers from his childhood.

] _

He pauses, looks around, and begins to write a simple program, remembering just enough BASIC syntax to put the computer into an infinite loop displaying the same phrase over and over again. *There is so much more to see. Not the newest additions and especially not the addition to the addition*[1]. He wishes he had more time in the museum before needing to get back to the train station. He would have liked to have written something more interesting here.

---

[1]there are two things the Mathematician despises, both this and the other, burn his eyes to the soul, bone to the marrow

Chapter 16

2.39996322972865332...

August 18, 2018

Another train. A much longer train. An infinitely long train. A six and a half hour long train ride. It went fast, and thoughts were focused on designs and optimization problems: poisoning the castle's troops and protecting th' pieces of eight.

He enjoys the castle and gardens in *Northumberland*. He enjoys them immensely. The dukes. Too many tragedies. Stone swirls in the ponds. He wishes he would have eaten something from the other place. He enjoys the tour on history. So much history still untold. He enjoys the one on film. The past and the contemporary displayed simultaneously here and in film. He smiles hopeful. He wants to watch Beckett again. He thinks, and then rethinks: "The second, second king?"

August 19, 2018

Another important date. This was really the first, not the second. On the second night, he's moved to another room, the room just above the den. The noise doesn't seem to bother him, he's falling asleep on the bed. This room has a couple of books that pique his interest. One is a book of collected works of a somewhat local author. One is a volume of old stories he can't remember. He thinks of the ironies here. He thumbs through the pages and one of the stories catches his eye.

> Il lit à propos de l'erreur laissée dans les instruc-
> tions sur au angle.

He thinks of the program he left on the computer at the museum, still running in an infinite loop.

He reads this story from the book, a story that he had never read before, and enjoys it thoroughly. He has a copy at home that he keeps next to the two, ten pound boxes of chocolate (the contents long since eaten), a Mexican wrestling mask, a Wolverine action figure (still in the box), and a pennant flag proclaiming him the world's best dad (caption: dadie helping me do my homework).

August 24, 2018

A new day, a new beginning. He loves thinking about math. More than half the day. Some days he tries to maintain his train of thought for the entire day. The same problem. Working the problem from different angles. Working related problems. For some reason, especially around this time of year, cryptically, but surely coincidentally, yet seemingly every year, at this time of year, he has significant breakthroughs in thought.

He wonders if the breakthroughs for this year are over. He wonders if there might be another. He wonders about future breakthroughs this time of year. He wonders about the time of year. His thoughts turn to his family. He misses his wife, his children, especially his youngest daughter.

His trip has taken him away for two months. He looks forward to going home. He doesn't look forward to the journey: the two-hour train ride, the half-hour train ride, the eight-hour flight, the shuttle ride.

He breaks his train of mathematical thoughts around lunchtime. He usually skips lunch and works straight through. He decides that he shouldn't toil away *this* day entirely thinking about mathematics. He thinks about going back to the Pub. He's staying above an old pub. *Did I already say I was staying above an old pub?* He thinks about the other two times he's stayed above an old pub, one pub claiming the same being true for a famous sailor or the author of the same. He can't remember which. Maybe it was both. He tries to remember another claim, something he saw in The Dirty Bottles in *Northumberland.*

He tries to push these thoughts out of his mind and return to mathematics. But then he remembers seeing an ad on TV about a curse. Seemingly unrelated thoughts, but thoughts that he could trace back if hard pressed. He rushes to a market, buys two kebabs because he can't make a decision—and goes to the rented flat to see if he can still catch part of the show.

An episode is playing on TV. It's not the show he wanted,

but it's close. The other show strikes a chord with his childhood memories. He hasn't heard of this treasure, but he fondly remembers hearing about the other. He thinks of crazy notions of quitting everything and taking his family on a hunt for treasure, searching for beauty and only finding a beast.

. . . .
. . . .
. . . .

Chapter 17

The Halos

September 11, 2018

Suddenly the Mathematician's thoughts are back in the present. He looks down at one of the pieces of paper on his desk. It's a drawing of a head which appears to have two halos over it. *Are those halos?* He looks at the clock, wondering where the time has gone.

9:20

He looks at the digital clock. 9:20. He can't read analog clocks. *The days at school when they must have been covering analog clocks and calendars—those days my family must have taken me out of school, probably in the process of moving or something. No real correlation here. Just happenstance. How often did the Captain have to move his Angel?* To this day, the Mathematician has never been comfortable with time, dates, and arithmetic.

99

The Mathematician moved a fair bit .... at least when he was younger. He doesn't think it affected him much, but he's probably wrong. *Is this rational or transcendental?* He himself, as a father, has only moved his family twice. His kids have enjoyed the stability. His father's occupations couldn't afford this. He draws more patterns, some real, some coincidences. He again turns his thoughts to Angélique.

9 : 20

He reads this as a date: 9-20. Another important date. *The hour is young.* He wonders how he is going to mention the 28th of July and then realizes he already has. He also sees that it's not nearly as late as he thinks. He thinks positively of this. His wife won't be too annoyed at putting their daughter to bed by this time. He remembers his wife repeating, "Don't forget to put your daughter to bed." He remembers hearing it twice but wonders if it was twice. 9:20. In about two hours he thinks his wife will come home and that they will watch a show together. The second season of a much-anticipated series they were watching had just come out. He needs to spend more time with her. He wants to write; he needs to write to empty his thoughts. But he knows that he's been obsessing since he returned from his trip.

He has to take time off from work. He will lose it otherwise. He loves work, but he loves his family, but has an obsessive focus. He rationalizes that this is what makes him a mathematician and that this is what provides for his family. He knows he's rationalizing but he believes it.

He can obsessively focus for days. He has, in fact, obsessively focused on the same two math problems for 20 years. On these problems, he has made some progress, more progress than he is ever willing to report, but no real solutions yet. His thoughts go to Hardy, then to Ramanujan, and then back to Turing.[1]

Before his wife leaves, he makes a promise about writing up his most recent breakthrough, a breakthrough that he can actually share with her; she doesn't really want to hear it but knows he wants her to hear it. A breakthrough he can share with the world. He promises it won't take long and that he won't obsess so singularly. He thought of presenting his findings as a research paper. She says "No. No one will read it. Tell it like a story. Let the readers find the clues."

He loves doing math. He hates writing. Well, he loves writing code. His mind again sees another meaning in this. He intends to write the word programming. He loves breaking codes. He decides to write the word ciphers instead of codes. He leaves the text unchanged because he enjoys the irony of the situation. He didn't like writing ciphers. He looks back and sees another meaning. Then a few he didn't even intend. Would that be a problem? He doesn't like breaking code. A contradiction wrapped up in an enigma? He enjoys the simplicity and complexity of this statement.

He at once realizes he has been too revealing. *Allowing access into one's thoughts is dangerous.* He also thinks he must be in the first few lines of an infinite loop in a live demo. He tries to interrupt his thoughts. He wonders if

---

[1]Hardy was an English number theorist who famously, and incorrectly, said that number theory was a study without any practical applications; Ramanujan was an Indian number theorist who evaluated many infinite series and provided solutions to mathematical problems considered unsolvable; Turing was an English mathematician, computer scientist, and cryptanalyst who worked at Bletchley Park and helped break the Enigma cipher

the museum curator knows how to interrupt the loop he left running on that computer. *Did he have to reset it?* He wonders, even now, if he has referenced that computation. He worries about the damage that will be done to the old monitor. He looks up and notices his old monitor and the time that the digital clock now displayed.

Success. He feels as if he's broken out of his infinite loop. He again looks up to the digital clock. 9:26:53. This is definitely not a date.

Part V

The Tale

Chapter 18

The Curse of Oak Island

September 11, 2018

The Mathematician is now putting his daughter to bed. He reads *Beauty and the Beast* to her. He sees no immediate pattern here. He looks briefly for one but then turns his thoughts elsewhere. He kisses her on the head and tells her to go to bed. Now he sees it. He tells her that he loves her and that she should go to sleep. He draws parallels back to Angélique, and this motivates him forward. He uses this opportunity to grab another can of soda from the downstairs refrigerator.

The previous week, when he should have been preparing for his family's return from their vacation in a small cabin in the woods, he had become obsessed with the *Curse of Oak Island*.[40] Well not the curse, but the cipher he saw on the TV show. His family would still be away for a couple of days. He started watching every episode of the series on streaming TV. He thinks it took four days. He was working during the day, watching Oak Island at night. With his family absent, he would normally be working all available hours. He is still tired from his trip. His family returns, and he pauses his progress and focuses on his family. He misses them so much. He enjoys the hectic chaos they bring. He might have just dug himself into a hole.

He experiences a few down moments when his wife wants to read. A few hours here. A few hours there. The progress on Oak Island increases exponentially. Then before realizing it, he is obsessively researching everything. His wife realizes this and makes her best attempts to interrupt his focus. He subtly increases his children's interest in the show. His little angel now calls it the *digger show*. He immensely enjoys watching the series with his children and tries to encourage them as their interest wanes. He convinces his wife of the family bonding opportunities it presents. He purchases the most recent episodes, and he begins to watch the revelations at a feverish pace.

He now feels that he is brought up to speed. He is seriously doubtful about all of the present theories concerning the Money Pit and Oak Island. He easily finds serious flaws in all of them. William Kidd had no treasure to bury. The Templars wouldn't bury religious relics in the wet Money Pit and leave them unguarded. Shakespeare's works left to disintegrate in the earth? Burying the French crown jewels, by someone who needed the money and not recovering them?[105] Yet the more he watches, some kind of evidence seems to be mounting. Suddenly, although he cannot yet explain how, he knows that something must have happened on Oak Island.

He tries finding the simplest explanation that fits with all the details. The most plausible theory was some kind of old tomb to a revered person or persons, given the 18th century human bones that were found in the Money Pit. Again he could find flaws in this thought process. Perhaps all of the clues have anecdotal or incidental explanations. This would, of course, be sufficient but his mind saw that too much complexity would be necessary. *This can't be right.* He begins to resign himself to the next season of the show. He then hears rumors that the network wants another season of the show but that the Lagina brothers were private people and were not sure. This is how they left the season. The Laginas and their partners have literally invested millions into the Money Pit. Evidence is starting to mount, but nothing seems definitive. Nothing seems to fit perfectly. There are surely too many flawed theories and crackpots proposing more.

His middle son wants him to go on the Curse of Oak Island show and pose as a crackpot. His son tells him to start the conversation explaining how his "expertise comes from raising monkeys in Oregon."

He knows that he's not a crackpot. The field of mathematics is probably even better suited for crackpots and dispatching them quickly. In mathematics, you can easily read a purported proof until you find the first mistake, point it out, and then dismiss it entirely. There are so many purported proofs that they build up. Occasionally a proof by a respected mathematician appears. These proofs are checked by others with rigor. Usually, small flaws are found. Most are easily fixed and do not take away from the approach. Occasionally there is a death knell. An obstruction.

He stops abruptly and worries about the similarities in his present undertaking. He thinks of Einstein and how he was so sure of his theories that he pointed out tests that could be made. *Surely these claims can be easily tested and refined.*

In mathematics, you may be able to prove something definitively. You may also be able to assume its truth and derive new understandings. His thoughts turn to another Hypothesis. His thoughts turn to a Theorem. A Theorem that might have been concluded much earlier had the publisher left more room for the author. He smiles at this and then pushes this thought out of his mind completely. He returns back to the subject of this text. Now back to the Hypothesis, then to subtlety, then realizes he can develop them both and make more progress. This moves him forward.

Entire libraries of thought built on a simple observation, and then generalized even further, fitting very little data. Like a substitution cipher without enough entropy to decipher it... Yet the hypothesis is simple and elegant. The search for supporting data grew exponentially after the hypothesis was published—well as long as such growth can be sustained. *He thanks more for this.* He knows you will see spelling errors or maybe a grammar error; maybe both. He leaves the typos. Now, most mathematicians believe the hypothesis, are ready to assume it, thrilled if it leads to a contradiction, or are at least convinced that it is effectively true. As far as we search, the evidence holds up. His thoughts turn again to Hardy, but this time to Littlewood[1].

"What does it mean to prove something?" He asks and answers. "It means that a reasonable person that believes in

---

[1]Littlewood was an English mathematician who famously proved a very reasonable conjecture verified up to the first 10^{14} instances was, in fact, false—the first counterexample being somewhere around 1.397162×10^{316}

and follows the same assumptions and guiding principles will reach the same conclusion regardless of the course taken."

His thoughts turn to a packed lecture hall at a conference on number theory where the infinite series

$$\sum_{n=0}^{\infty} \frac{F_n}{2^n}$$

was *proven* to be transcendental, with all of the complexity of numbers like $\zeta(2)$ and τ. The speaker was the celebrated Dutch number theorist. The Mathematician remembers, at the very instant he saw the series, thinking to himself that it's algebraic at best. Binet's formula says so. To this day, he wishes he would have instantly shouted out, "Surely, it's algebraic!"

He grabbed the back of his conference agenda and quickly proved to himself that it was rational! He did some easy computations, and if his algebra and arithmetic were right—he doubted only one of the two—the infinite series was integral! He knows that you might not know the value, but that you could.

He verified his computations by the end of the talk and went up to the speaker, still at the projector. He waited until the other mathematicians finished asking their questions and then quietly went up to the podium, the speaker still at the projector gathering up his slides, and showed the famous speaker his simple calculations on the back of the conference agenda. The speaker quickly saw the same simple outline of the proof and conceded, a bit flustered. "I thought we checked that," the speaker told him.

Somewhere in the speaker's very complicated proof, there was an insurmountable error. The simple approach written on the back of the agenda said so and both he and the speaker, both being reasonable, agreed. The speaker's line of attack was surely correct; his theorem was surely sound. His theory just didn't pertain to this particular example; some small error had been made.

Perhaps, in the Mathematician's current venture, just as in physics, a theory concerning Oak Island cannot be proven. Or, at least, not to the degree of detail desired by the Mathematician. Perhaps evidence will just continue to mount in its favor. Some small issues may be found, but, just as in mathematics, these should be easy to fix and not take away from the simplicity and elegance of the solution. In physics, we know that solutions are approximations. We know that theories, even laws, are continually refined and corrected. As theories are developed, we learn more, and the endeavor opens up new avenues of testing and refinement.

10:22. His wife comes home. "How did putting our daughter to bed go?" "Good." "Do you wanna watch our show?" "Sure." The letters in the title of the show remind him of Ockham's Razor: a philosophical principle that the best explanation is the simplest, the one with the fewest assumptions. *Is that the right spelling of Occam's?* He realizes just now that he hasn't been drinking his drink. Upon editing this last line a second time, he realizes that this is still true. He decides on the subtext for the title, rereads the entire text, and then goes to bed. At least, right before this, he does a double take and looks at the time. It's 3:14!

Part VI

The Wire

Lavoir Entendu et leüe sa derniere volonté
avant Mort, au Louveaux Le 8è de ...
May mil sept Cent Quarante en presence
des Sr François Leconte Escuyer Sieur de
Nouville Chr de l'ordre militaire de Sr Louis
Lieutenant du Roy et de honoré Bertin
Chirurgien Major des troupes de Cette
Ide de Cayenne lesquels qui ont avec led.
Testateur signé a ces Cet escrit faite

à pour Estre placer Cher les pauvre de la
Congregation de Cette ville;

+ Item Led. Sr Testateur a dit qu'il laisse
Veut et entant que les tapisseries et les
Tableaux et la ferme alle du gouvernement
soient attachez au Gouvernement +.

Item led. Sr Testateur a dit qu'il laisse
Laisse au Sr Bigot Comme ... Onze volumes
du dictionaire de morery le pnière de l'avaquer

+++ Comme aussy veut Led. Testateur qu'il soit
Executeur testamentaire ...

Chirurgien ... autres personnes qui sont soigne
et traite y en sa ... sa maladie

[signatures]

Chapter 19

A Few Good Dispatches

Forant,

Sieur d'Espiet is dead. Du Chambon, son of the King's lieutenant of Île St Jean, has been appointed in his place. It has become necessary to relieve Saint-Ovide, Governor of Île Royale since April 1718. With good grace, we would like to extend this position to you. Concerning promotions, we rely more on talents, zeal, and application than on seniority, which is why I will send every year an annotated list denoting the qualities and defects of each candidate.

— Maurepas
1739

Maurepas,

I humbly refuse the position of Monsieur de Saint-Ovide which you have offered to me...

— Forant
March 19, 1739

Forant,

The King intends that you accept the position of governor of the Île Royale which is offered to you.

— Maurepas
April 3, 1739

Forant,

As governor, we will constantly send you provisions. You must begin boarding your furniture at once...

— Maurepas
April 14, 1739

Beauharnois[51] and Hocquart[56],

The former Governor of Île Royale having asked permission to withdraw from the service, he was replaced by Forant as governor of Île Royale. Mr. Le Normant having been transferred to Cape Town, Mr. Bigot, Commissioner of the Navy, was chosen to replace him.

— Maurepas
May 12, 1739

Forant and Bigot,

Enclosed you will find instructions concerning the reforms I wish you to enact.

— Maurepas
May 26, 1739

July 1, 1739 Saint-Ovide, captain of the King's ships and former governor of Île Royale, hereby leases to Isaac Louis Forant, captain of the King's vessels and new governor of the said island, his dwelling with all his apartments and outbuildings located in the bottom of the harbor of Louisbourg Bay, for the sum of 500 livres a year.[18]

Maurepas,

I acknowledge receipt of the governor's provisions and am ready to leave on the Jason.

— Forant
July 16, 1739

Maurepas,

I have conferred with Forant on what concerns the government of Île Royale. I deplore the false accusations that have harmed me in your eyes.

— Saint-Ovide
July 28, 1739

Maurepas,

I am writing to inform you of the arrival of Forant and Bigot, gentlemen on the Jason, commanded by Mr. de Vaudreuil...

— Sabatier
September 14, 1739

Maurepas,

None of the complaints brought by the soldiers against their officers were found substantiated.

— Forant
November 14, 1739

May 7, 1740

Maurepas is already done with Governor Forant. It hasn't even been a year. Maurepas would receive Forant's November 14th letter in the late winter. Maurepas expected the governor to enact the reforms the Grand Conspirator's suggested and carry out his requests. The governor refused. The governor refused to remove the officers the Grand Conspirator desired for removal. Forant sided with the officers and found the allegations reported by the Grand Conspirator to be unfounded. Maurepas was not to be refused. Maurepas sent at least two dispatches that would arrive in early Spring of 1740. The dispatch to the governor we have no doubt about. The other would have been to the Comptroller.

To Governor Forant, the Grand Conspirator wrote "It would seem that you are determined to let them continue to exist... I cannot give my approval to the position you have taken on this question."[43]

To the newly appointed Comptroller, the Grand Conspirator would have related something advantageous to both the Comptroller and the Grand Conspirator; something advantageous to port Île Royal; the means to furnishing better appointments.

May 10, 1740

Forant was dead. "An inflammation of the lungs."

September 15, 2018

The Comptroller will relate that Forant became severely ill in late April. Perhaps after Bigot received instructions from Maurepas and began administering the Minister's deadly prescriptions. The Comptroller will write glowingly of the governor's qualities and had the governor buried beneath the Chateaux Saint-Louis chapel.

The Mathematician reads online:

> When he made his will, Forant was obviously in the final agony, judging from his six labored attempts to affix an adequate signature. After bequeathing to his colleague Bigot his eleven-volume set of Moreri's Grand dictionnaire historique and to the governor's residence his tapestries and paintings, which were numerous and of fine quality, he asked that something be given to his domestics and those who had assisted him in his illness. In a gesture which was unparalleled in Louisbourg's short history, he stipulated that the residue of his estate be used to provide eight bursaries for the education at the Louisbourg convent of the Congréga-tion de Notre-Dame of daughters of Île Royale officers. After some disagreement on the part of Forant's sister and only heir, Marguerite de Forant, to whom Bigot had sent her brother's

furnishings, a compromise was reached in October 1741, whereby the sisters would dispose of 32,000 livres from the estate, while the residue was awarded to Mademoiselle de Forant. The following year, in June 1742, the fund was invested in France at 5 percent per annum.[43]

A last will and testament made at the hands of the Comptroller? Made when Forant was either too weak, or entirely unable or unwilling, to sign his name? Or was it a complete forgery by someone without much practice? Problems with six attempts at a signature? Bequeathing property to the Comptroller and to the Port, while only knowing them for 8 months, having not even wanted the appointment in the port at all, while having a living heir, and after just refusing to carry out the orders of Maurepas? The Comptroller and the Port standing to gain immensely with the death of the governor? The true heir in astonished disagreement?

forant forant forant forant
forant forant forant forant
forant forant forant forant
forant
forant forant forant forant

forant forant forant forant forant
forant forant forant forant
forant forant forant Forant

Chapter 20

Another Dispatch or Two

October 3, 2018

The Mathematician studies the last will and testament and it is clearly forged. The early attempts are severely misshapen and appear to abort at spelling mistakes. The Mathematician finds many consistent signatures of Forant during the last year of Forant's life. Even the final attempt at a signature on the last will and testament looks nothing like any of Forant's signatures. The forged signature looks nothing like what one would expect even in an impaired state. The overall pressure, size, and flow is not consistent with Forant's signatures—though strikingly consistent with Bigot's signatures. The F has completely the wrong basic shape, is done in two movements instead of one, has too small of a loop on the top and a unique extra loop on the left, and the angles and curves don't match. The O is too wide. The R has a slight loop instead of the typical tight v shape. The A is not wide enough and not consistent with the shape of the O. The top of the N tilts down instead of up, and the bottom doesn't go down to the baseline. And the T—the T transcends comparison with any of the other samples, especially with a unique upward extension coming to a rest instead of the consistent purely horizontal extension from one of two positions gliding off the paper.

October 4, 2018

The Mathematician tracks down the notary, Laborde, who notarized the last will and testament of Forant, the fraudulent forgery of the Comptroller. For his part in dispatching with Forant and his possessions, the Notary was granted a "property on the Rivière de Miré (Mira River), acquired in part by official grant as early as 1741, now stocked with 12 cows, a bull, and two horses, forming three métairies (share-cropper's properties) and a meadow." Laborde's notary services would turn out to be continually useful to the conspirators. Laborde would acquire a great deal of wealth, including several privateering vessels, "two houses in Louisbourg, one of the finest fishing establishments in the harbour including a warehouse measuring 80 feet by 30 feet and a lodge big enough to house 80 fishermen," hundreds of thousands in livres, and would be made Treasurers General of the Marine and Colonies where his embezzlement of 455,474 livres would eventually catch up with him....[37]

Maurepas,

I am ready to embark...

> — *Mr. Duquesnel,*
> *governor, replacing*
> *Mr. de Forant, deceased.*
> *September 19, 1740*

The Mathematician attempts to determine the timeline of events and concludes that arrangements for Forant's replacement were well underway before the announcement of Forant's death. Maurepas was well aware of the time it took to arrange a replacement. Duquesnel was appointed commandant and given all the authorities of governor without the title and had already begun making arrangements for his new life in Louisbourg and was transferred at first opportunity to replace Forant. The Mathematician discovers that Maurepas will use these same tactics again in 1747, in the case of the Marquis Jacques-Pierre de Taffanel de La Jonquière and Marquis Roland-Michel Barrin de La Galissonière—Jonquière as Forant, Galissonière as Duquesnel—although Jonquière will escape the attempt on his life when Maurepas's plan goes awry.

August 22, 1742

> Judgment of the Council of State by which His Majesty approves and confirms so much the foundation made by the late Sieur de Forant, Captain, Governor of Île Royale, eight places of boarders at the Sisters of the Congregation of Louisbourg for of daughters of officers, that the constitution which was made over the clergy of France of a pension in the principal of 30,000 livres. (M. de Forant had bequeathed all his possessions for this object, his sister pretended that he had not had this right since his property came from his mother, and that the Will established a mutual substitution between them. There was a compromise, and it is this compromise that the King confirms by this judgment.)[19]

As it would turn out, Duquesnel, too, would soon be dispatched after refusing to follow Maurepas's orders, this time from Duquesnel's refusal to refrain from attacking the British.

Maurepas,

I regret to inform you of the sudden death of Mr. Duquesnel and ask you for his place...

— Du Chambon
November 10, 1744

The Comptroller's friend, Louis Du Pont Du Chambon would become acting governor. Du Chambon's brother, Michel Du Pont de Renon, was married to Marie Anne De Goutin in 1710 and died in a drowning accident on September 4, 1719. Marie Anne would later marry Michel Hertel de Cournoyer, subdelegate of the intendant for Port-Dauphin, Nova Scotia, in 1724. Cournoyer will become the acting bailiff in 1744. Upon de Renon's death in 1719, the family leadership devolved upon Du Chambon. In 1737 Du Chambon replaced D'Espiet de Pensens as king's lieutenant of Île Saint-Jean. D'Espiet, neighbor to the Reyniers in Bordeaux, was handpicked by the Grand Conspirator's father to serve with Sabatier and the De Goutins on the Superior Council of the colony. D'Espiet was similarly involved in the same illicit dealings as the other conspirators. The Du Ponts were a military family who treated Port-Dauphin as their personal fief and were among the military officers most active in trade. Cournoyer as the bailiff, would provide Bigot even more opportunities to increase his volumes of collected works, maybe even from the widow Chevalier's estate.[15, 46, 47, 64, 71, 72]

The Mathematician finds it difficult disentangling the widow-many-times-over Marie (Louise) Anne De Goutin (Desgouttes, Saint-Martin, Baudry, Bochet, Duquesne, Beaulieu, ...), daughter of an Île Royale officer, sister of the Comptroller. The Comptroller's sister seemed to be collecting the pensions of multiple husbands after their deaths. Perhaps she was even enjoying the endowments from the posthumous Forant foundation established by her brother. With her multiple marriages and husbands with multiple surnames, she might have even been eligible for all eight of the available stipends.

We know much of Du Chambon's role in the surrender of Île Royal to the English and very little of Du Chambon's eventual replacement except that the replacement was so late in arrival, that he never arrived. We also know, from both historians and contemporaries, that "Forant's achievements were sufficiently positive that he would have made a difference in the mutiny and siege which his immediate successors had to deal with"[43] and that Duquesnel "would have almost certainly prevented the mutiny which occurred only two months after his death."[34]

Part VII

The Shut-Out

Chapter 21

Profitable Undertakings

January 29, 1743

The Grand Conspirator could see the Cardinal's grip slipping. The Cardinal's clenched fist relaxed, and his hand opened. The crown, while not actually in the Cardinal's hand, still fell, as if it were, to the ground. The breath first, then the spirit, left the Cardinal's countenance. Cardinal de Fleury was dead.[90]

A few weeks later...

The Grand Conspirator walks across the Fontainebleau palace gardens. He is accompanied by a man dressed in noble attire. The two begin their conversation by exchanging pleasantries.

After the formalities, the Grand Conspirator is quick to take control of the conversation and relates the details of an incredible undertaking. The Grand Conspirator then begins with what, to the other man, seems like a history lesson.

"Louis XIV died in the year one thousand seven hundred and fifteen. Louis XV was then five years old. Maurepas was fourteen. Louis XIV wanted his favorite son, however illegitimate, to rule France..."

"The Duke of Maine?" the man interrupts, hoping to impress the Grand Conspirator.

"Yes," the Grand Conspirator continues, giving an expression of disapproval, clearly annoyed by the interruption, "Shortly before his death, Louis XIV rewrote his will to restrict the power of the soon to be Regent, Duke of Orléans, the renowned soldier and braggart of crimes."

The Grand Conspirator pauses, testing the man's sense of decorum, giving the man an opportunity of repeating his earlier mistake in interrupting Maurepas. The silence approving, the Grand Conspirator continues, "The changes would allow the Duke of Maine to rule with a Regency Council of fourteen members until Louis's 13th birthday. Decisions were to be made with a majority vote and..."

"Meaning that the council could vote out Orléans?" interrupts the man, now looking apologetic.

The Grand Conspirator, appreciating the brilliance in the question, decides not to admonish the man for breaking decorum and simply continues, "Orléans, seeing the trap, immediately goes to Parlement after the King's death and annuls the very will of the King. In exchange for Parlement's support, Orléans reestablishes Parlement's *droit de remontrance*, the right to challenge the King's decisions.[1] Orléans seizes power and essentially rules France until 1723. Louis's tutor, the Cardinal, becomes his confidant and advises Louis

---

[1] The Mathematician cannot help worrying about the order of these two operations

to appoint his cousin, Duke of Bourbon, to replace Orléans as prime minister. The Duke of Bourbon essentially rules France until 1726 while the Cardinal continues to gain the King's influence. Beginning around 1726, the Cardinal's ascendancy is complete. For the last 17 years, the Cardinal has essentially ruled France, spreading his religious persecution and diminishing the power of Parlement. But now the Cardinal is dead."

The Grand Conspirator looks to the man, now encouragingly, entreating the man to ask the obvious question.

Finally appreciating the situation, the man asks, "What now?"

"Ricouart," the Grand Conspirator continues, tightening his fist, "Ricouart, now, we must seize this opportunity before the King is drawn into the clutches of another. When the War of Austrian Succession first started, do you remember the King's response?" The Grand Conspirator takes on the mannerisms of the young king, places his hands in his pockets, and attempts to mimic the King's voice, "In these circumstances, I don't want to get involved at all. I will remain with my hands in my pockets, unless of course they want to elect a Protestant emperor."

"Stupid as the peace," adds Ricouart, "Working for the Prussians...."

"The Cardinal would focus on diplomacy while Louis focused on science," the Grand Conspirator continues, "The Cardinal remained determined to downplay the importance of the Navy. With Maurepas in one ear and the Cardinal in the other, Maurepas slowly gained more and more influence over the King. The King would see the growth in the foreign maritime trade and the hundreds of millions of livres that could be taxed. This growth needed protection. Maurepas would convince the King of the grandeur that the Navy could attain, the success in the war that could secure the King's legacy. The King's fancy is now wearing thin, and he is now being seduced by *more attractive offerings.* For the last few years, the King has now taken three mistresses, the Queen having been counseled by the royal doctors to take a respite from having relations with the King, after the loss of an unborn child. The King, feeling rejected, has not been to her bed since. The King began looking to bed elsewhere. The King found it first in his court with Louise Julie de Mailly, and then by her sister Pauline-Félicité de Mailly. Pauline de Mailly became pregnant by the King, but both mother and child died in birth. The Cardinal took this opportunity to call the King to repentance saying that these unfortunate events were the result of the King having turned to adultery, refusing to go to confession and take the sacrament."

"So the King turned to religion for consolation?" asks Ricouart.

"Yes, until he became *full of the spirit*," quips the Grand Conspirator, proud of his wit and delivery. "Louise Julie de Mailly unwittingly introduced the King to her youngest sister, Marie Anne de Mailly."

"All three sisters?" asks Ricouart, "The King having all three?"

The Grand Conspirator, pauses and then answers, "Yes, having *spent* all three—choosing an entire family—is that being unfaithful, or constant?"

While the Grand Conspirator is saying those last three or four words and just as Ricouart is beginning to laugh, the King, seemingly from nowhere, catches up with the gentlemen still walking through the gardens. The King, with a sense of urgency, places himself directly in front of the Grand Conspirator, catching Ricouart in total surprise and the Grand Conspirator in mid-sentence.

"Being faithful and constant," the Grand Conspirator smoothly redirects the conversation, "Your Excellency, recall if you will, your faithful and constant servant, Louis Balthazar de Ricouart, Chevalier, Seigneur d'Herouville and de Villeroy, steward of the Navy in Rochefort, brother of the Comptroller in Île Royal."

Ricouart, the laughter instantly withdrawn, bows his head slightly and makes a motion with his hands, indicating sincerity. The King glances at Ricouart, gives a brief acknowledgment, the honesty of which neither the Grand Conspirator nor Ricouart can read.

The King, still full of urgency, turns back to the Grand Conspirator. "The Duke of Noailles has just shown me this letter," the King says, handing the letter to the Grand Conspirator. The Grand Conspirator feels caught off guard, his mind racing with thoughts of what the letter could contain.

"A letter," the King continues, "that my great grandfather wrote to his grandson."

The Grand Conspirator immediately relaxes and visibly sighs with relief, betraying the Grand Conspirator's usual composure. The King, noting the Grand Conspirator's response, becomes distracted by this.

"Yes, of course, the—letter," the Grand Conspirator says, trying to regain his confidence, "Yes, a letter that must have been written by King Louis XIV to King Philip V of Spain."

The King, now reinterpreting the Grand Conspirator's

earlier response and finding it much less intriguing, continues. "Precisely, it counsels," the King, taking back the letter, begins to read, "don't allow yourself to be governed; be the master. Never have a favorite or a prime minister. Listen, consult your Council, but decide yourself. God, who made you King, will give you all the guidance you need, as long as you have good intentions."

"Excellent, Your Excellency," the Grand Conspirator replies, "I couldn't agree more. Speaking of this very counsel, this is exactly why I have brought Ricouart, the overseer of Rochefort, here to Fontainebleau with utmost urgency. Sire, the expenses of the Navy are foreseen to be even greater than the last year."

The King turns away, "Jean... Jean... Jean. In 1739, I granted you an extraordinary budget, more than doubling the expenses of the previous year. 20 million livres..."

"No, your sire," the Grand Conspirator interrupts, "It was only 19 million livres: a mere £826,087."

Ricouart interjects, "19.2 million livres."

Both the King and the Grand Conspirator look at Ricouart reproachfully. Ricouart shrinks in stature and takes a step back.

"Jean, you are, indeed, the spinning-cat," says the King.

"Spinning-cat?" asks the Grand Conspirator.

"Diane Adélaïde de Mailly," the King explains, "Marie Anne's older sister, has taken to calling you 'the spinning-cat'. Maurepas, quite content chasing the object of his own fancy, spinning in circles. It does amuse me so..."

"I'm sorry," the Grand Conspirator apologizes putting on an air of submission, "the spinning-cat was not aware that there was yet another de Mailly sister within the King's reach."

The King laughs and then gestures, "The King's reach is far, and that stretch of river may soon run even deeper between the two bends, but I, myself, have not yet fully made her acquaintance. She, like you Jean, is quite the entertainer. She lacks your intelligence, though. She insists that her husband has cheated on her, and so she's not even sure if she is the mother of her children!"

"Let's hope," the Grand Conspirator responds with a tone of sincerity, "that the Mademoiselle finds more profit in her future *undertakings*." The Grand Conspirator, giving the King no room to reply, abruptly refocuses the conversation, "Alas, this brings us back to the discussion of profits. You are right, sire, the amount was 20 million but the year was 1740, and the taxation from the maritime trade profits are projected to far exceed this. Our interests need protection, and we have already delayed too long in *these undertakings* that *are* necessary..."

The King interjects, "And was it not 26 million in 1741 and 27 million just last year? How can there be anything left to purchase? And what do we have to show for it? We have yet to discover the Northwest Passage that the natives keep telling us about. I would rather increase the funding of that expedition than continue this war."

"Your Excellency," the Grand Conspirator asserts, "the British Navy still outspends us nearly 2 to 1. Almost 90 percent of the British budget is spent on the War. Each year, they take in about 5 or 6 million pounds in taxes and spend about 7 or 8 million pounds on the war."

"Yes," the King concludes, "which means, just as we do,

that they go deeper and deeper into debt for this war; they who are willing to tax three times the rate we do; they who place a burden on the people with a debt 15 times greater per person than we."

"With serious risk comes extraordinary reward," the Grand Conspirator advances, "and even at 27 million livres, with 23 livres to the pound, compared to the British spending about 25 percent of the war budget on their Navy, we are still at a disadvantage."

The King, now sure of himself, responds, "Even desiring it so, Jean, our people will not stand for more increases to taxation, the ten percent tax on revenue is already highly unpopular, and our debt continues to grow. The paper promissory notes were a disaster, and the Church and nobles remain unfairly exempt from property taxation." The King, now much less assertive and much less confident, continues, "I'm thinking of abolishing the ten percent tax and establishing a 5 percent tax on all, including the Church and nobles. I'm considering issuing bonds to pay off this debt."

The Grand Conspirator decides to change his approach, catching the King somewhat off guard. "Excellent ideas, Your Excellency. However admirable these pursuits are, they will be met with great resistance; they must be done when your house is in order, when your interests are secure, and when the people are rejoicing in your victories. Let us first decisively dispatch the English and then reap the reward."

The King, now feeling a sense of hopelessness and with his guard down, resigns "We simply cannot afford your proposed expenditures, Jean."

"There is a way," the Grand Conspirator proclaims at once, finally arriving at his intended destination, "but let's discuss this later..."

That night, they would talk about price fixing; manipulating the beaver fur trade; privatizing as much of the naval operations as possible; giving benefits to the merchants such as tax concessions, special permissions, and increased convoy protection; the merchants like Jean Beaujon loaning tens of millions of livres to the crown in exchange for advantages in shipping and smuggling goods to America. They talked of sugar, tobacco and slaves. They talked of an even more profitable venture. The King was finally on board. Dispatches were made, and arrangements would soon be commenced. The Grand Conspirator began making even more arrangements. Arrangements that even the King wasn't privy to.

A Plan of the TOWN and HARBOUR of LOUISBOURG in the Island of CAPE BRETON.
Taken from y. French on June 17. 1745 by y. New England men under y.
Command of General Pepperell, assisted by y. British Fleet: command-
ed by Admiral Warren.

Rivulets wher ships may Water

autre Aiguade

Habitations

THE   PORT

Lake

a Rock under Water

A Scale of 500 Toises

Entrance of the Port

A. Town of Louisbourg
B. Casern or Lodging Room
C. Pond or Water where the
   Fishing Boats are kept
   during the Winter
D. Stages on which they

dress and Salt the Cod
before they dry them.
E. Battery of 20 Cannon
F. Battery of 30 Cannon
G. Battery of 40 Cannon
H. Battery of 8 Cannon

to defend the Preceding one
I. Battery of 24 Cannon
K. Battery of 15 Cannon
L. Battery of 40 Cannon
M. Battery of 15 Cannon

Chapter 22

Best Laid Plans

The preparations take nearly three years. The foundations had been laid much earlier, but the Grand Conspirator was just now seeing his life's work come together: a house so noble once erected would never be subject again.

With every turn of the screw and strike of the hammer, the conspirators grew closer; the *maison noble* grew stronger. Maurepas's pride swelled greater by the moment. Each motion of the artist was by itself, a masterfully crafted work of art, but the composition as a whole was a masterpiece, worth incredibly more than the sum of its parts, a creation so flawless even the Creator would be jealous.

The work of the conspirators made them all increasingly invested. There would be no turning back now. The King saw the labor as an investment. The conspirators only looked to the conclusion. The final strike would be made, a fatal blow with a finishing thrust so unsuspecting and so complete, leading to the ultimate coup de grâce.

Maurepas had arranged for the King to send an unprecedented amount of money to Canada for the construction and fitting out of ships, for paying ransoms and bribes; a purchasing power so complete and so damaging to British interests that it would alter the course of the colonies forever.

£2,000,000 were to be transported on the King's massive store ship, *La Gironde*, at the end of May 1745, or commencement of June at the latest, destined for Île Royal. Four powerful warships would accompany the ship to ensure its intended destination. A convoy of merchant ships would provide a distraction if needed.

Convoys provided safety in numbers. The less valuable ships could flank *La Gironde* and provide distraction and escape for the treasure ship. If the fleet were attacked, the warships would form a line of aggression, ultimately sacrificing themselves if needed, providing the time required for the convoy to escape.

The profitable undertakings suggested by the Grand Conspirator had all been approved, and the totality of those undertakings succeeded in creating a fund necessary and sufficient for manipulating the King's path to victory.

What the King didn't know, is that moments before the King found Ricouart and the Grand Conspirator talking in the garden that day at Fontainebleau, the Grand Conspirator had just finished relating an elaborate plot to steal this fund right out from underneath the King and to use it to bankroll the efforts of *La Grande Société*. £2,000,000 in the hands of powerful merchants would create a power that rivaled that of the King.

The Grand Conspirator personally selected the crew of the treasure ship and passengers that were to be granted transport. The Grand Conspirator arranged for a new vessel to be constructed in Quebec. This vessel was the appropriately named, *Le Castor*, meaning *The Beaver* in French. The command of the vessel was to be given to Pierre Morpain, a privateer, port captain, and naval and militia officer. Morpain had a reputation that exceeded his works and ability. He was feared as the dreaded "More pain."[70] Morpain was a double agent, also working for the conspirators. Morpain was to proceed to Louisbourg to rendezvous with the treasure fleet.

Morpain, after the rendezvous, would take charge of a crew of 200 midshipmen and proceed to Quebec to take command of *Le Castor* with the midshipmen as his new crew. *Le Castor* was to be loaded with 50 tons of beaver pelts. Before the official commencement of the War, the conspirators arranged for the West Indies Company to significantly raise the price of beaver while holding the price of other goods constant. The artificial escalation in the value of beaver and the price fixing of other commodities would create a significant revenue source for the French, pass the cost onto the British, and allow for beaver to be effectively exchanged for the effects of war at a very advantageous rate.

The 200 midshipmen were to be transported on a merchant ship from St. Malo to accompany the treasure fleet. In early March, 25 soldiers were recruited to serve as crew on the merchant ship. The crew, like the midshipmen, were deemed expendable.

The stop and return to Louisbourg were designed to enable the fleet to pass by the Bay of Gaspé where a separation from the fleet was to be arranged. Hiriard and Sallaberry were to captain *La Déesse* and *L'Andromède*, respectively. The warships and other convoy were to be detached from the rest of the fleet except for *La Gironde*, the treasure ship, and *L'Heureuse Marie*, the merchant ship carrying the 200 midshipmen and Morpain, and Hiriard and Sallaberry's ships. Ultimately, the route to Quebec would be deemed impassable, and in the Bay of Gaspé, an even more elaborate set of measures were to be taken to separate the King from the treasure.

To help cover up the plan, *La Gironde* was to be packed with as many munitions of war as possible, under the pretense of arming privateers. Privateering was to be encouraged a few months before the commencement of the plan. The King would never know what hit him.

The captain of *La Gironde*, Le Gardeur de Tilly, was seen as too loyal for taking part in the conspiracy. The conspirators needed insiders on the treasure ship to ensure its separation from the fleet and its derailment into the bay. The Grand Conspirator arranged for the advancement of Charles MacCarthy (Latouche).[1]

MacCarthy was made post captain at La Rochelle and captain of the port of Quebec, taking the position held by Morpain, who was to take command of *Le Castor*. The conspirators also perceived Morpain as being expendable.

MacCarthy, once onboard the *La Gironde*, was to take control of the ship from Le Gardeur de Tilly, perhaps by poison. The Grand Conspirator had been perfecting the art. First Forant, then others, and most recently, just a few months earlier, the King's mistress, Marie Anne de Mailley, who was arranging for a public humiliation of Maurepas for spreading knowledge of the King's *ménage à trois* with the de Mailly sisters on the battlefield in Metz.[75, 102, 103]

---

[1]MacCarthy might be Bigot's nephew—both are referenced as sailing on the Léopard, and there is an Irish connection to the Ricouarts.

MacCarthy was given a salary of 1,000 livres and the rank of lieutenant of frigate. For his role, MacCarthy wanted more and wrote the Grand Conspirator requesting a change in the arrangements. The Grand Conspirator would promptly write back:

MacCarthy,

I can make no change in the arrangement for your position as captain at the port of Quebec, and if you think you will not accept it on the footing stated, you will kindly let me know.

— Maurepas
April 22, 1745

MacCarthy, valuing his life and reading clearly into the subtext, would accept the original terms of the arrangement.

The Grand Conspirator also arranged for Le Vasseur to be sent back from his internship on *La Gironde*, as another insider on the treasure ship, an insider granted special permissions and authority. Le Vasseur was also to play a critical role in the happenings that were planned in the Bay of Gaspé.

In late April, news of the activities of the Comptroller and Du Chambon in Louisbourg began prematurely interfering with the mission. The Comptroller was ahead of schedule in his efforts to surrender Île Royal. The Comptroller had been making life miserable for the soldiers, withholding their pay and providing them with spoiled goods while selling fresh provisions to the populace. The English were notified that the port was ready to fall. The Comptroller arranged for the officers to stand down in the attack and Du Chambon offered them pardons and monetary compensation for their roles. The British began a blockade, the premature timing of which, now interfered with the conspirators' plans. News of the impending attack was planned to reach France just after the treasure fleet had left, not before.

The Comptroller not only interfered with the precise timing being orchestrated by the Grand Conspirator but also kept insisting on installing grain mills in the colony that would interfere with Jean Beaujon's profiteering. *The Comptroller needs to become privy to more of the arrangements, for he will otherwise become more of a wrench in the works.*

With the treasure ship unable to enter Louisbourg and Morpain unable to rendezvous with the crew of the 200 in Louisbourg, other arrangements had to be made. Morpain was out, Dubois was in. Briand Dubois, a ship captain in St. Malo, was to just proceed directly with *L'Heureuse Marie*. Dubois was to be given sealed orders to open at sea to accomplish the role that Morpain was to play.

Dubois,

> *You will not open the sealed orders that I send you, until several leagues to the west of Ouersant. You will proceed direct to Quebec with* Le Castor *seeing that the English are to attack Louisbourg. You will send to Beauharnois and Hocquart the letters for Du Chambon and Bigot, and if you are attacked by a superior force, you will throw the packages into the sea.*

> *— Maurepas*
> *April 24, 1745*

On May 20, 1745, Dubois and the crew of *Le Castor* are already well underway to Quebec, having left from Brest.

On May 27, 1745, Le Gardeur de Tilly had recently become uncomfortable with the small crew arranged for his voyage and requested an increase. The Grand Conspirator, having carefully selected the crew members and its size, had to deny its increase.

On June 3, to explain the loading of the money and the tonnage it displaced for other goods, iron bars are reported as needing to be transported in the cargo of *La Gironde*.

The King having heard the rumors of the imminent attack in Louisbourg sent orders from the Camp below Tournay instructing *La Gironde* to sail at once to provide relief and to save Louisbourg.

The King's new target of the expedition was no longer compatible with the conspirators' plans to steal the King's money. Already more than two weeks behind their scheduled departure, the crew of the 200 on the merchant ship already on their way getting further and further ahead, and the money still not having been loaded, the Grand Conspirator is forced to call off the plan.

> *Ricouart,*
>
> *You may dispatch* La Gironde *without waiting for the money intended for Île Royale. Send Bigot the flour he asks for...*
>
> — *Maurepas*
> *June 18, 1745*

The window of opportunity was closed, and the conspirators found themselves completely shut out. All that remained was for the Grand Conspirator to ensure that *La Gironde* sailed without the money so that the conspirators would have time to design a new plan and inform the other conspirators that new arrangements had to be made.

> *Barrialt,*
>
> > *The news received from England renders the departure of the convoy more and more urgent... As the season for navigation to Canada and Île Royal is already advanced, you can, if not yet ready to leave, order M. de Tilly to sail alone with the vessels he is to convoy.*
> >
> > — *Maurepas*
> > *July 22, 1745*

> *Ricouart,*
>
> > *We will have a new agreement with the Sr. Simon La Pointe, for the charter of his vessel L'Andromède, for Canada, her voyage to Île Royale having become unnecessary.*
> >
> > — *Maurepas*
> > *July 22, 1745*

Part VIII

The Sting

Chapter 23

Try, Try Again

The Grand Conspirator replayed his failure over and over in his mind. He berated Ricouart for the delays.

Ricouart,

The King is much displeased at all the delays that have taken place in the departure of La Gironde.

— Maurepas
August 23, 1745

The officers and soldiers of Île Royal were eventually transported to France. Bigot and Du Chambon were required to give a falsified account of what transpired. The Swiss regiment in Île Royal was blamed for the surrender. The King became intent on interrogating and punishing the soldiers. The Grand Conspirator, on the other hand, would arrange for the matter to be dealt with quickly, by a court-martial of his appointing.

155

The officers were now worried about what the soldiers might say, justly implicating them in the conspiracy. Some of the incriminated began dying in the hospital and prison. In a November 26th letter to Barrialt, the Grand Conspirator arranged for only the sergeants and corporals who actually took no part in the revolt to be interrogated, leaving the officers aside. The surrender being dealt with, the Grand Conspirator returned to studying his failure.

The critical failure in the Grand Conspirator's plan was in the timing. *La Gironde*, being the King's ship, was subject to the delays inherent in organizing the King's expeditions. The merchant ship carrying the 200 midshipmen was able to leave on schedule. In the Grand Conspirator's next attempt, he would see to it that the treasure be sent on a merchant's vessel.

The next failure to be addressed, also related to timing, was in coordination. Coordinating the communications between the conspirators in France with those in Canada with up to a four-month round trip delay was excruciatingly painful. Orchestrating the conspirators' activities in the earlier plan required precise timing. The Grand Conspirator would build more fail-safes into the new plan.

The King, facing the recent embarrassment of losing another stronghold in the colony, was now bent on seeing the funds transported and commencing with the operations to recover his losses. The King urged secret preparations to begin. The Grand Conspirator was to ready an extraordinary squadron with multiple battalions of troops. The expedition was to leave shortly after March. Hundreds of ships were to be prepared (20 warships of the line, 21 frigates, 32 transports, hundreds of merchants in convoy). 3,000 soldiers, 10,000 marines and 800 cannons were to be delivered in an amazing show of force.

The hundreds of merchant ships were to be escorted in one of two convoys, depending on their desired destinations. Some of the merchant ships would proceed with the main expedition and others would go under a convoy with Hubert de Brienne, Comte de Conflans, protected by 4 warships of the line. Conflans would first offload ships in Martinique, then Santo Domingo, and then secretly rendezvous in the Bay of Chebucto[1] with the main force. The Grand Conspirator ordered these preparations to be done with a great deal of discretion. He also ordered 3,400 rifles to arm all able-bodied men in Canada.

The main expedition to recapture Louisbourg, Plaisance, and Port Royal was to be led by the Duc D'Anville, Jean-Baptiste-Louis-Frédéric de La Rochefoucauld de Roye, the Marquis de Roucy. The dukes of La Rochefoucauld belonged to one of the most influential and noble families in France, going back to the 10th century. Going back as far as the 16th century, the dukes were nearly all named François. After François XI, the family had no male heir. By letters patent by the King and the Pope, the title was transmitted to the male issue of Duchess Marie-Louise-Elisabeth de La Rouchefoucauld on the condition that she marry a member of the La Rochefoucauld family. She chose her distant cousin Jean-Baptiste. The Duc D'Anville had minimal naval experience and lacked proper training, but was nevertheless made Admiral and given command of the French fleet.[9, 44, 120]

The treasure would now depart, not on the King's ship, but on a merchant ship under the convoy of either Conflans

---

[1]Halifax, Nova Scotia

or Duc D'Anville. The conspirators seem to make early provisions in the event of either of these two outcomes. Early in the planning, Conflans's convoy appears to be preferred for the treasure ship. However, by April 30th, the Grand Conspirator writes to the Judges and Counsuls at Nantes that "the prodigious number of vessels (now numbering 214 merchant ships) that are being placed under the protection of the convoy of the Chev. de Conflans, produces too much talk and it will be well to take other measures." The alternative is to send the treasure ship with Duc D'Anville's contingent. The conspirators would have to detach the treasure ship and have it arrive ahead of the main expedition. The Grand Conspirator informs the Duc of the additional merchant ships in his convoy and letters are exchanged in preparation.

To fix the timing issue, Sallaberry and the Hiriards would winter (hunker down) in the Bay of Gaspé or by the Angels of the Island near Newfoundland. In doing so, the Captain, the Pirate, and the Engineer would already be in place with half of a new crew of 200. The treasure ship, with the Sculptor and the other half of the new crew, would only need to rendezvous with the other ships. The Captain would patrol the entrance to Quebec and intercept the treasure ship on its final leg to Quebec. The Pirate and the Engineer would be anchored at Oak Island, ready to see to the operations of actually separating the treasure from the King.

Sallaberry would leave first, delivering communications with the Canadian conspirators and leaking both real and fabricated intelligence to the Americans and the British. In fact, the colonials in America would receive the same letter from several different sources, the "merchant Iriard" being the most reliable.[39] The merchant ship, being much smaller than *La Gironde*, wouldn't be able to carry the required amount of crew and incendiaries. *Looking back on it, carrying the treasure and the incendiaries on the same ship was not the brightest of ideas. But combining the treasure and as much of the crew of 200 as possible in one ship was brilliant.* The merchant ship carrying the treasure would be nearly completely laden with coin. Hiriard and Sallaberry would take the remainder of the required crew and as many munitions and gunpowder as they could, and these would be transferred to the merchant ship after the treasure was unloaded.

The Grand Conspirator would inform the King that Hiriard was an expert at navigating the St. John River and could transport munitions from there to be distributed to the Indian nations to assist in the ground offenses of the war. This provided Hiriard with a reason to sail way in advance of the main fleet to arrange for the supposed distribution of munitions. Sallaberry would transmit the much-needed intelligence (and the intentional misdirection) and then claim to be patrolling the mouth of the Saint Lawrence for English activities.

In reality, the new and ingenious design of the Grand Conspirator solved the crucial timing issue, while also providing a reason for the Captain's schooner to be armed for war and a reason for provisioning the conspirators with the incendiaries they required. The Pirate and the Engineer would already be in place to oversee the details of the exchange, and the Captain would be ready to intercept the merchant ship before arriving in Quebec.

The conspirators' merchant friends, the Gradises, would provide a merchant ship sufficient for transporting the treasure. The treasure ship would be *Le Fort Louis*. The ship would be captained by François Drouilhet, associated with the conspirators through business dealings. Drouilhet would ensure that *Le Fort Louis* detached and sailed ahead of the fleet and secretly rendezvoused with the Pirate and Engineer. The merchant ship would carry half of the required crew of 200 to play the same role previously intended by the crew of *Le Castor. La Renommée*, the fastest ship in Duc D'Anville's expedition, captained by Guy François de Kersaint, was also given the task of detaching from the expedition and arriving early, providing protection if needed to *Le Fort Louis*.

The plan was proceeding as intended, this time, with very few hitches. On June 17th, the Grand Conspirator sees by a letter from the Duc D'Anville, that after passing the Capes, the Duc proposed to allow the merchant vessels going to Canada to proceed alone. While this could make the Conspirator's planning easier, it also introduced the possibility that the treasure ship could be taken by a privateer before the treasure was intercepted. The Grand Conspirator writes back to the Duc that "it seems to him desirable that he detach a frigate from his squadron to conduct them as far as the Strait of Belleisle." This frigate would be *La Renommée*, and cause no real issue with the conspirators' plans while providing protection until the treasure ship could be securely detoured into the Bay of Gaspé or the Island of the Angels.

With the treasure ship plans complete, the Grand Conspirator turned to a secondary issue. The King's extraordinary force headed to a certain victory: a victory so powerful and so complete that it would set back the Grand Conspirator's designs for years. The simple solution to crippling the King's expedition, while still providing what the King requested, rested in its sheer size.

The Grand Conspirator placed the Comptroller in charge

of overseeing the expedition's timely departure. The Grand Conspirator arranged for the ships to be outfitted at different ports. Duc D'Anville's flagship, along with many of the other warships, was to be outfitted in Brest. Jonquière was supposed to sail with the duke but would be transferred to *Le Borée*, the ship designated to transport the Comptroller.

The outfitting of the ships at different ports made it easy to target the vessels of the fleet that were intended to receive tainted provisions. Probably in the wine or flour or baked into the ship's biscuit, and probably $Pb(CH_3COO)_2$, a slightly sweet tasting poison, known to antiquity, that was readily available to the conspirators in large quantities. A company contracted to provide the food rations for the fleet was arranged to administer the provisions with debilitating doses of poison. *Le Fort Louis, Le Borée* and the other ships outfitted in Rochefort were not subject to the tainted provisions. Bigot and Jonquière were meant to survive the voyage and were given secret promotions—the Comptroller would become intendant and Jonquière would become governor—to be carried out upon their arrival.

The Duke and his second in command, Vice Admiral d'Estournelle, were to be ravaged by the effects of the poison and would be in no shape to continue the expedition. The command of the expedition would be given to Jonquière, the Rear Admiral. The voyage was destined to become a naval disaster, another crowning achievement for the King. The Comptroller, who proved himself in covering up the surrender, would be entrusted with all reports of the voyage.

As an added insurance policy guaranteeing the King's failure, one of Culliford as Sabatier's duties was overseeing the Mines near Trois-Rivières and the works at the Forges of Saint-Maurice. Sabatier had seen to it that the cannons produced in these forges, and used to help armor the fleet, were defective.

With the British governors—Shirley, Warren, and other distinguished people—having been made aware of *La Grande Société* intentions to poison the expedition, the British and Americans called off their response and ended their activities in raising up militias for defense. The treasure ship was to sail unmolested.

The only thing that would now interfere with the Grand Conspirator's plan was the lack of a timely departure, delaying the expedition into winter.

Ricouart,

I cannot hide from you how dissatisfied I am with the lack of diligence and attention on your part. I have ordered you to do precisely what M. Bigot and M. de la Brosse ask and it seems that you have only undertaken to gainsay them and delay everything. I don't know what your aim may be, but I warn you well in advance that any continuation will not be very pleasant. I should have thought that you might have profited better from a clarification that we had together at Fontainebleau, but all that has happened since in the port doesn't give me leave to believe that you remember it as well as you ought. For me, I assure you that I do remember and I will remember.

— Maurepas
April 1, 1746

Image ©2018 DigitalGlobe. Google Earth.

Chapter 24

The Money Pit

Sieur Chéron, commanding *La Société*, manages to leave a couple of days before Hiriard. Chéron left Rochefort on the 6th of March, 1746, and arrived in the colonies on June 3rd. Chéron delivered letters from the Minister and informed them that Sieur Hiriard was to sail two days after him, freighted with powder and other ammunition and merchandise.

Sallaberry, the Captain commanding the schooner *La Marie*, left Rochefort on October 16, 1745 with 30,000 pounds of powder and about 600 muskets. Sallaberry found himself on the gulf on the 6th of January and anchored at St. Peter's islands. The severe weather and other accidents obliged him to go back to Martinico, where he arrived on the 20th of February. He remained at the islands where he had his vessel re-caulked. He could have sailed early, but for fear of the English privateers who were known to be in the passages. He was obliged to wait for the convoy of a privateer that was armed; they sailed in company on the 20th of April. It was only under cover of a battle which the Frenchman gave an English privateer, that Sieur Sallaberry escaped. Sallabery would meet nothing after that. Sallaberry arrived in the colonies on June 6th. Sallaberry also delivered the Minister's letter on the first of November of last year.

Hiriard, the Pirate commanding *La Déesse*, left Rochefort carrying 30,000 pounds of powder, about 400 muskets and various munitions of war around March 8th, 1746. He sailed from the Île d'Aix on March 24th. On April 6th, he was forced into Ferol for repairs and left on April 27th. On June 25th, Hiriard arrived at Ille a Rassade. He disembarked an express to inform the colonies of his arrival and to send copies of letters previously received. On July 4th, Hiriard anchored *La Déesse* in the road-stead of the expedition.

Drouilhet, commanding *Le Fort Louis*, the 350-ton treasure ship, left from Rochefort charged with carrying the King's shipment. *Le Fort Louis* was supposed to leave La Rochelle in March or April, but, thanks to Ricouart's efforts, or lack thereof, didn't get underway until June. The loading of the treasure and artillery train was done in secret. *Le Fort Louis*, carrying £2,000,000 and half of the required crew of 200 with their rations would have been nearly completely laden. The other half of the crew and any heavy equipment or extra supplies would likely have been carried in advance by Hiriard (including a proportion of the 200 pick axes and 200 short handled picks that were ordered for the expedition, along with a variety of other tools like saws, shovels, etc.).

Kersaint, commanding *La Renommée*, also charged with the mission of detaching from the fleet and staying with *Le Fort Louis*, arrived in Beaver Harbor ahead of the expedition on September 4. Kersaint sheltered there, purposefully avoiding the original rendezvous point of Chebucto Bay.

Drouilhet, according to Maurepas's memoirs, never stopped, sailing past the main fleet who lost a lot of time in the Azores, waiting for favorable winds. The treasure ship, now detached from *La Renommée* and continued to sail past Chebucto. The following is from a ship's or captain's log that was eventually recovered by the Oak Island researcher, Doug Crowell.

September 6, 1746

Enter a deep bay southwesterly of Chebucto Bay. Still no word of D'Anville and the weather being clear we set sail turning southwesterly along the coast past many rocky islands. At midday, we reach a deep bay with several hundred small isles wooded to the shore. The wind dying down we anchored for the night. The great quantity of treasure on this vessel makes it unwise to jeopardize it in any engagement with the enemy.

September 8, 1746

It has been agreed that a deep pit be dug and treasure securely buried, the pit to have a secret entrance by a tunnel from the shore. With 200 men, we estimate work can be finished in ten to fifteen days. Soil seems free from rocks. Work begun on pit twelve feet in diameter. Slow progress.

September 9, 1746

Thirty feet down, no rock. Thirty men employed. Lookout at mouth of bay has made no report of sail.

September 10, 1746

Forty feet down, cave-in and man killed. Buried at top of hill. Men now working in two sections. Others employed making timbers for supporting sides of pit and for tunnels.

September 11, 1746

... Sunday and very rainy. Pit filling up with water and loose soil. ... walls of pit supported by logs and timbers. Hauling rope used for hauling up earth ... and injured two men who were removed to ship.

September 13, 1746

Pit seems damp from seepage of sea water. Have decided to go deeper to dry soil. Soil not dry enough. Passed through a shelf of rock. Making plans for a secret tunnel ... chamber....

A treasure chamber off a long corridor from the Money Pit, passing under the marsh and terminating near the middle of the island was constructed and the treasure was securely buried. Le Vasseur, being from a long line of master carpenters, had selected the location of the Money Pit: under a great oak tree. Oak was very important to the Le Vasseurs (the Le Vasseur descendents recently filed an official coat of arms where the oak tree plays a prominent role).[61]

Le Vasseur, on *Le Fort Louis*, was given charge of the King's money and was the insider placed on the treasure ship to help convince the other crew of the necessity of burying the treasure, having not heard word of Duc D'Anville, having lost the protection of convoy, and fearing for the treasure's protection. Le Vasseur, helping allay concerns of the crew should an accident befall the expedition, used the few weeks on Oak Island to leave clues. Le Vasseur proceeded to artistically employ his talents in sculpting and his knowledge of runes for encipherment to ensure the treasure could be recovered.

Runes were important to woodcarvers and sculptors and would have been studied by Le Vasseur. The Mathematician suspects that Le Vasseur left other carvings, most notably the cross and tobacco for instance, at other locations as *Le Fort Louis* sailed around the area. Le Vasseur constructed a simple cipher and left etchings in flagstones and on boulders and made an elaborate system for decoding the treasure's location: *la formula*, a formula for discovering the Money Pit and the treasure chamber. He left the so-called 90 foot stone, not at ninety feet as claimed by later treasure-seekers to gain funding to continue their excavations, but with the other flagstones near the surface of the pit.

The Pirate used this opportunity to symbolically bury his leather bound, parchment bible in the pit, not being able to reconcile his future actions with his past repentance and forsaking of sin.

The Engineer was instrumental in the construction of the pit and its draining mechanisms and used the coconut coir he obtained in the West Indies to help with the efforts.

Maurepas claimed that *Le Fort Louis* managed to anchor in Chebucto Bay on September 17th with the other ships. The Mathematician is not convinced of Maurepas's timeline, but if the 10-15 day estimate was accurate, then it might have been possible. On the other hand, they might have just checked in on the 17th, fearing they were becoming overdue. In any event, their next corroborated whereabouts took place on October 15th, when Drouilhet attempted to ignore orders to proceed to Quebec and stay behind (since his mission was to proceed to a rendezvous with Sallaberry). Drouilhet was forced to continue with three other merchant ships to Quebec under escort by *La Renommée*. Note this was an unintended consequence of Maurepas's earlier request caused by the delayed departures and separated arrivals.

Le Fort Louis was escorted to the mouth of the St. Lawrence. Maurepas, attempting to justify the following, noted that "the four sailboats were beaten by the gales, easily predictable in this season much too advanced for the navigation of the river. Presumably, none of the ships could reach the capital of Canada." This is contradicted by all of the other ships, which attempted entry, having made it to Quebec during the same time period, including the three other merchants and the Hiriards' ships. The only ships that claimed issues were Sallaberry's in his part of the cover-up (he claimed both of the ships he sailed encountered issues, possibly explaining the missing ships or missing cargo under his stewardship).

Maurepas, continuing his fabricated account but now under an entirely different pretense, related: "The fate of Gradis's ship is known to us through a memorandum written by his shipowner. Fort Louis had taken on a leak, and Drouilhet, renouncing the return of the St. Lawrence, set sail for the Islands of America. He was attacked at the sight of Santo Domingo by three corsairs, defended himself as best he could and, at the end of his resistance, took the 'jiarti' to make his ship fail, so that the effects of the King, of which he was concealed, did not become the prey of the English; he himself escaped by gaining the coast at night and swimming. The same fatal fate struck the whole expedition of the Duc D'Anville. An epidemic of scurvy exterminated the soldiers and the sailors. The squadron, unable to attempt any attack, returned to Brest and left for Rochefort. The storm and the disease had more mutilated than big defeats. Anville was dead. Gradis solicited the minister to indemnify him for the sinking of *Le Fort Louis*. Maurepas recognized that a compensation seemed fair to him, while asking him, before taking a decision, a detailed statement noting the object of the loss."[50]

The Mathematician discovers a second account which doesn't place *Le Fort Louis* with the other ships in Chebucto Bay until September 27th. "Loaded with guns, cannon balls and other cargo partly for the State, partly also for its owner, David Gradis, the ship left Bordeaux on April 13, 1746, for the island of Aix where he arrived on the 15th. Sailed for Quebec in the Duke of Anville convoy on June 22 and arrived in Chebucto on September 27, where 45 warships and merchant ships were anchored. Escorted one day by the frigate, Renommé, it raises the anchor for Quebec with the Sultane, the Virgin of Grace and the Andromeda on October 15th. Damage caused by storms forced him to tack on October 19, so he took the direction of the West Indies. On November 19, three British corsairs after a two-hour battle caused him to fail near the French Cape in Santo Domingo. The captain reaches the French Cape on December 13th. On May 5, 1747, he resumed the sea for France as captain of the Wheel of Fortune. She is captured two days later and driven to "Yorck, New England". The captain was exchanged at Leogane on July 14, 1747. Again at the command of another ship, the Theodore de Nantes arrives in France on December 1, 1748, where on January 6, 1749, he reports to the Admiralty."[2]

Part IX

Cover-Up

nor myself one of prayr allow, as i saild.

i'd a bible in my hand, when i saild when i saild,
i,d a bible in my hand, when i saild,
i,d a bible in my hand, by my farther,s great command
But i sunk it in the sand, when i saild,

j murdered william moor, as j saild, as j saild,
j murdered william moor, as j saild,
j murdered william moor, and left him in his gore.
Not many leagues from shore, as i saild

And being cruel still, as i saild, as i saild
And being cruel still, as i saild,
And being cruel still, my gunner i did kill
And his precious blood did spill, as i saild

My mate was sick and died, as i saild as i saild,
My mate was sick and died, as i saild
My mate was sick and died which me much terrified.
When he called me to his bedside as i saild,

And unto me did say see me die see me die,
And unto me did say see me die

Chapter 25

Dead Men Tell No Tales

Three may keep a secret, if two of them are dead.

— Benjamin Franklin
Poor Richard's Almanack, 1735

The King, of course, didn't believe Maurepas's story. The King would continue to investigate the incident and refuse Gradis's compensation for years. The level of Gradis's involvement is not clear. Evidence of how persistent Gradis appealed for his small compensation of loss compared to the losses the King concealed, is evidence that Gradis might not have been aware of the details of the operation.

On the other hand, Gradis's appeals might have been a perfect pretense to seem unaware. The King, being very intelligent, would take note of a shipowner not requesting this indemnification. In any event, it would be hard to claim that Gradis was unaware of the future operations of the conspirators, in which he was heavily involved.

In truth, *La Déesse*, a snow and a schooner (possibly Boucher and Sallaberry, possibly Boucher's son) would return to Quebec after loading *Le Fort Louis* with incendiaries. Under the excuse of providing relief to the forces at Chebucto, the Hiriards and Sallaberry would rendezvous with *Le Fort Louis*.

Drouilhet in *Le Fort Louis*, knowing full well that his orders forbade him entering Quebec, proceeded to the designated rendezvous and left the mouth of the St. Lawrence after *La Renommée* left. Sallaberry's departure would be slightly delayed by the ice and either alone, or with the Hiriards having doubled back, would have rendezvoused with *Le Fort Louis*.

The details that follow are not entirely clear. Aubert, Arbour, and Chicouanne, three residents and lookouts for the British near the bay of Gaspé, reported seeing what was surely *Le Fort Louis*, continually tacking, purposefully not making any progress, from November 24th to early December, contradicting the captain's account that the ship was already at the bottom of the ocean on November 19th. The ship continued making signals near the shore attempting some kind of rendezvous (hoisting its white flag, firing a signal, similar to the other secret signals used in the associated ground expeditions of the Duc D'Anville mission). *Le Fort Louis* repeatedly anchored there, every night, and finally sailed on December 3rd. *Le Fort Louis* "fired one gun, hoisted a white flag and shoved out her broadside, the wind bearing north, the Cape wearing southeast, and disappeared."[39]

The crew of the 200 would have been combined, by some pretense, on *Le Fort Louis*, now heavily laden with incendiaries. They would have sailed out of sight, presumably to deep ocean, possibly as Maurepas indicated heading toward Santo Domingo, and the conspirators, most likely Sallaberry and possibly the Hiriards, would have blown the entire ship to pieces leaving no survivors.

Chapter 26

A Le Vasseur at Rochefort?

Le Vasseur, having previously switched ships from the ill-fated *Le Fort Louis*, briefly visited his family in Quebec before leaving with the other conspirators to France and resumed his work for the King in Rochefort. This presented many issues. There was an official record that Le Vasseur sailed with the King's treasure on *Le Fort Louis*, and his parents unwittingly continued attesting to his internship and brief return, and yet Le Vasseur somehow survived the terrible mishap at sea that claimed the entire ship, save the ship's captain. The Conspirators would spend years covering up Le Vasseur's trip.

The King was anxious to put Le Vasseur back to work and might have hung a threat of prosecution over his head, suspecting his involvement. Le Vasseur was effectively a prisoner in the King's workshop until just before 1760 when Great Britain would, unknowingly, arrange for Le Vasseur's release. Le Vasseur's sculptures after 1760 and before his ultimate disappearance in 1769, would secretly, but now finally, be monuments and memorials for the 200.

Pardevant les No.res a Loüisbourg
Isle Royalle soussigné present, en personne
Messire Charles Dailleboust Cheur
Ch.er de lordre Royal militaire de S.t
Louis Lieutenant de Roy en cette Isle
Messire Deganne Cheur Sieur de Falaise
Ch.er de lordre Royal militaire de S.t Louis
Major des troupes et de la place
de cette ville et S.t Trezorteme et p.re
Capitaine aide-major de cette
ville y Residans Les quels ont
par ces presentes declaré reconnu
par ferme que en Dellib.n amoureuse
que de la Communauté d'entre feu S.t
Macquee Degoutin de son vivant escripuis
argendemaganin au fort Royal en l'acadie
et de dame Jeanne Thibaudeau conjoints
Il me resté de x Enfants vivants ou
Enfants Representans, que S.t François
Marie Degoutin Concl au Conseil
Superieur de cette Isle, S.t abraham
Degoutin Directeur, anne Degoutin
veuve de M.re Bernon et Courroyer,
decedé en l'anne 17 by quarante S.t
et dont elle a laissé dept enfants d'p.re
Leur Communauté vivante, Demoiselle
Marguerite Degoutin Espouse du S.t de
Sessemy officier de la maison d'la Reine
decedée ayant laissé de x l'a laute ville
Sa Communauté, S.t Joseph Degoutin
Notaire Residante a la nouvelle orleans
a la Lovisiane, Demoiselle Jeanne
Degoutin veuve de feu S.t de Nouberlebel
de Meauveur Cheur Capitaine aide-major
en cette Isle, demoiselle Magdelaine
Degoutin Espouse du S.r pierre Boucher
Ch.er d'lordre Royal militaire de S.t Louis

Jnjumon du Vya Callipte decedée
en Samen mil Sept Cents quarente Sçe
ajant laisse quatre lé Saut Suivans
de Sa Communautte, et demoiselle ——
Louise Degovim veuve de feu S.' Ramor
Paul Sabatier Brunam dlamarine ——
en Cette Jle, et quela Son melfieur ——
Jaemem et antone Begotim freres ——
font morts Sans hoirs vujaut point ——
ette mariés de laquelle declaration ——
Attestation et affirmation led.' Boucher
y present avoir Signée Cette Cigne
ture po.' Rejaux Lurique avoir
octroye pour luy Servir et valoir Cequé
de droit fait aud Loumsbourg Clude
dlaborde hun denam laadrejupem ——
aud Loumsbourg apres midy le Douzem
november mil Sçe Cent Cinquant Set
me teret par Comparant Signes apres
lecture faite ;

Dailebourt   Desanu
   Boucher
                          Leppins
Laborde   moim n.a.d.

Chapter 27

Settling the Accounts

Culliford as Sabatier was commissioned with "settling the accounts of Île Royal". The Mathematician saw, in the Canadian Archives, details of this ongoing affair with much more emphasis and work than it deserved. Sabatier, having effectively retired, would have no place in doing this simple and menial task. Suddenly the task became clear to the Mathematician. What this meant, was tracking down people with first-hand accounts of the conspiracy and killing them. Culliford as Sabatier, a pirate with blood already on his hands, was well capable of silencing conspirators that could no longer be trusted or more conveniently seen as expendable. Culliford would rather be a party to the silencing than the silenced.

Maurepas, like always, began making additional arrangements that Culliford and other conspirators were not privy to. Maurepas makes attempts at collecting the conspirators together, their families and valets,[1] to receive awards, giving gratuities to the women and children who stay in France (en-

---

[1]valets were manservants or personal attendants

couraging the separation of the women and children from the men because he only intends to kill off the husbands and valets). He assures principal conspirators like Bigot of their continued engagement and indemnification from the silencing. He designates ships for the conspirators and their valets on voyages designed to intercept already alerted British fleets (MacCarthy's vessel containing the conspirators' valets being the most heavily attacked—valets being privy to conversations and letters with information that could harm the conspirators).

Of the principal conspirators, Culliford is killed first, shortly followed by Paule Sabatier, and then François-Marie De Goutin—the patriarchs seemingly killed in seniority order. The writing would seem to be on the wall for the younger conspirators. The other De Goutins and Boucher appear to fake their deaths and go into hiding.

The entire De Goutin family and all representative heirs were reported as being dead by 1750, some having already given power of attorney to the state relinquishing any rights to inheritance, in notarized letters by knights commissioned to track down their whereabouts. Jonquière and MacCarthy were nearly killed but somehow survived.

Maurepas had already arranged for Jonquière to be replaced before Jonquière even left on his doomed voyage, insisting Jonquière's replacement not reveal this promotion until the news of Jonquière's capture was official. Maurepas had even reported Jonquière as having been captured before the news surfaced of his escape. Maurepas even chastised Jonquière for fleeing the battle. Jonquière clearly suspected Maurepas's maneuvering. Maurepas was insisting that Jonquière set sail in a very narrow window of time, completely discounting and downplaying the eyewitness reports Jonquière was hearing about an English fleet sailing right towards the intended route.[121]

Conspirators with no apparent first-hand knowledge of the location of the Money Pit, like Sallaberry, seemed to be spared after his fellow conspirators made appeals on his behalf.

With very few left alive now knowing the location of the treasure chamber, the Oak Island money appeared to be secure. Bigot now begins a massive money laundering operation that continues for more than 15 years, with several business partners, companies and fences.

One of the more interesting parts of this arrangement has to do with the cannons Bigot seemed to steal from *Le Borée* at the end of the Duc D'Anville mission to armor the new company's ship, and the associated cover-up of this activity. The business partnership lists an explicit provision for returning said cannons to Bigot before the ship is to be refitted, presumably to prevent someone noticing the King's marks.

In 1749, Maurepas was removed from power in a coup and exiled from Paris for an epigram concerning the King's new mistress and advisor at court, Madame Pompadour. Maurepas would return to power only upon the King's eventual death and the beginning of the reign of Louis XVI.

Boucher, seems to give up sailing in 1752-1753, fakes his death, and puts on an eye patch and begins playing the role of Bigot's valet.[38, 59, 83, 84, 118] Boucher has a mysterious 9-month voyage right before he gives up sailing where it is possible that the remaining money could have been moved to provide easier access. There is mention of a storage facility that Bigot rented which could have stored the money.

On the other hand, the conspirators might have felt that the treasure chamber was the most secure place to keep the majority of the money and only returned on the rare occasions they needed. At least, for some period of time, it appears that money is withdrawn from the vault like a bank, as needed, in what the Mathematician now refers to as *Oak Island Banking*, surely ending by the early 1760s.

Shortly before 1760, Bigot's favor from powerful nobles began eroding, and he quickly became the scapegoat for the financial woes of France's tanking economy. Bigot was arrested for corruption and profiteering and imprisoned at the Bastille. It is not at all a coincidence that Bigot's downfall and the end of *Oak Island Banking* corresponded with Le Vasseur's release. In the final months of 1759, France suffered significant defeats to the British and lost Quebec. With Quebec gone, and Montreal surely falling next, the end of the war would soon be approaching, and France would be forced to cede New France entirely. The King would quickly have no need for Le Vasseur's services, and the conspirators would soon be unable to continue their operations. The death of King George II and commencement of the reign of King George III on October 25, 1760, also further, albeit very indirectly, complicated the activities of the conspirators.[95]

Bigot's trial would take years, and his fall would bring down many in power; the ordeal would end in a "78-page essay in scandal, printed and circulated in hundreds of copies, announcing Bigot's banishment forever, the confiscation of all his property, and the heavy fines imposed on all the condemned men. For perfidious officials who seemed to have plundered a colony and lost it to the enemy, the observing public would, in general, have been pleased with the torture and death recommended by the prosecutor on 22 Aug. 1763. A clerk in one of the bureaux of the treasurers general of the Marine wrote to a friend on 22 Oct. 1763, 'The gentlemen from Canada have not yet had judgment rendered, this is [due], it is said, at the end of the month; it is true that they were sentenced by the public a fortnight ago, Monsieur Bigot [to have] his head cut off, and Péan and Cadet [to be] hanged....'"[38] Bigot was ordered to pay back the crown over 1.5 million livres in restitution.

"At the same time, the public scandal of Bigot's corruption made it easy for the crown to treat most of the paper credit instruments from Canada as tainted and so to justify reducing them in value. Even the suspension of these instruments, the delays, and the necessity for the holders of such paper to apply to the government saved over 18 million in paper never officially reported. By 1764, there appeared to be paper to a total face value of over 83 million livres consisting of more than 49 million in bills of exchange, 25 million in currency notes, and nearly 9 million in notes receivable issued in Canada and never converted into bills of exchange. Ultimately, the total reached nearly 90 million livres of which the crown recognized only 37,607,000 livres, but it could not pay even this sum and so converted it into bonds bearing interest at 4 percent per annum, a rate of interest at which the French government could not borrow on the money market. Bigot may have cost the government something during the Seven Years' War, but the cost was largely in paper credit notes that were subsequently reduced by more than half and merely added to the long-term debt, the debt that was to bring the crown to the brink of revolution."[38]

Part X

X Marks the Spot

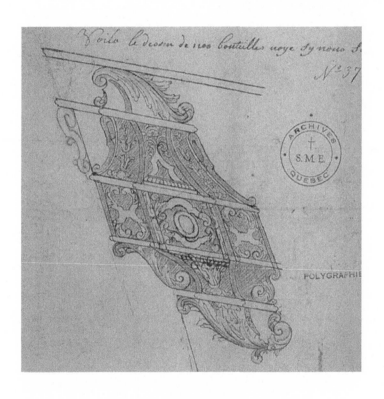

Voilà le dessein de nos bouteilles *noye sy nous f...*

N° 37

ARCHIVES
† S.M.E.
QUEBEC

POLYGRAPHIE

Chapter 28

Aftermath

Much of the remaining story of Oak Island is well known, and the Mathematician means to only touch upon those aspects relevant to the proof of this account. The Mathematician is lacking evidence needed to precisely recover much of the recent details where the record has trailed off. These details can doubtless be found with a more in-depth look into microfiche, further translation work, continued excavations on Oak Island, and even by taking a fresh look at the evidence found so far. The Mathematician feels that he has sufficient proof to justify all of his claims and prefers to leave a more rigorous proof of an even more detailed theorem to the enterprising reader. In case the reader perceives proofs as boring, and as a spoiler alert, the Mathematician has purposely deferred at least two of the most exciting aspects of the Oak Island story to the end.

prient dieu quil puissent estre de quelque

utilité, et d'avancer mes voeux pour votre ――

santé et prosperité estant

Monsigneur,

Chapter 29

The Maurepas Letters

Before continuing, the Mathematician would like to enter into the record, the following summaries of letters from Maurepas.

Ricouart and Barrialt,

> *The offer of the Srs.   Hiriard and Sallaberry, Canadian captains, to take* L'Andromède *and* La Déesse *from Rochelle either to the Baie de Gaspé or to that of des Anguilles in the island of Newfoundland, with all the arms and munitions they can take on board, to winter with these two vessels in one of these two places and to proceed at the opening of navigation to Quebec, is much liked by the King. We recommend that you push this expedition and concert measures with M. de Barrialt who is well acquainted with Canadian waters.*

> *— Maurepas*
> *October 21, 1745*

Simon La Pointe,

I have written to Ricouart concerning the use of your vessel L'Andromède *in the expedition proposed by Sallaberry.*

— Maurepas
October 28, 1745

Barrialt,

It seems extraordinary that they have not been able to find 200 men to compose the crew for the Srs. Hiriard and Sallaberry. You have done right, under the circumstances to accept the new proposal of Captain Sallaberry. I should have foreseen that my decision on the subject of the stay of the Sr. de Tilly would not be approved.

— Maurepas
November 1, 1745

MacCarthy,

Due to the stay of the La Gironde *not allowing you to proceed to Quebec this year, you will hold yourself ready to profit by the first opportunity that offers, next year.*

— Maurepas
November 1, 1745

Sallaberry and Hiriard,

I know the two of you to be moved by the zeal which has caused you to undertake your voyages to Canada. You will render a great service to the colony and can rely on the gratitude of the King.

— Maurepas
November 1, 1745

Beauharnois and Hoquart,

The loss of Louisbourg has been followed by other grievous events. Not only did the squadron arrive too late on the scene, but it had to return to France without accomplishing the other objects of its mission. The merchants have disarmed their vessels, and La Gironde has put into Rochefort. Under these circumstances, I send a schooner to Quebec loaded with arms and munitions. The Captain, Sallaberry, who commands her, counts on reaching Gaspé, thence to proceed to Quebec next spring on the breaking up of the ice. I will also send after the month of February two other vessels loaded with such supplies as will place the colony safe from any attack.

— Maurepas
Fontainebleau
November 1, 1745

Bigot,

I beg you to learn from the Sr. Hiriard if he knows no place on the Lower [side] which he can visit in March to go up to Quebec when the ice comes down.

— *Maurepas*
November 8, 1745

Ricouart,

The equipment proposed by the Srs. Hiriard and Sallaberry, not having been carried out, the King has approved the new proposals they have made. I presume that you have remitted to Captain Sallaberry the dispatches with which the Sr. de Tilly was entrusted for Canada. If you have not done so, you can retain them until first orders.

— *Maurepas*
November 8, 1745

Bigot,

Your prompt return to Rochefort is a new proof of your zeal. Your readiness to take up the expedition[1] of the Srs. Hiriard and Sallaberry is another. I hope there will be no delay.

— Maurepas
November 8, 1745

Ricouart,

... I have learned with great pleasure of the departure of the schooner La Marie, *commanded by the Sr. Sallaberry, and am pleased that you were able to give him the Sr. Vitré, whom he asked for as his lieutenant.*

— Maurepas
November 23, 1745

Ricouart,

The conditions of the Srs. Pascaud appear to be exorbitant, but in the present conjuncture, they must be accepted.

— Maurepas
December 17, 1745

---

[1] another translation gives *expiration*—both in hindsight turn out to be fitting. The French words seem sufficiently distinct that they shouldn't be confused, but the Mathematician has not been able to access the microfiche

Ricouart,

I approve the arrangement that you proposed for the fitting out of the vessel La Société, *of Île Royale, which is to be sent to Quebec under the command of the Sr. Chéron.*

— Maurepas
December 31, 1745

Guillot,

Maurepas desires to have 3,400 firearms, as well as 100 naval officers, sailors and cabin-boys required for the vessel they are building at Quebec, sent to Canada. As they cannot be forwarded by King's vessel, I beg you to see if you are not able to find what is required at St. Malo.

— Maurepas
January 25, 1746

Guillot,

You will charter the new vessel of which we spoke about for shipments to be made to Canada and for the passage of 100 men intended for the equipment of the frigate under construction at Quebec... You will hasten its departure.

— Maurepas
February 4, 1746

Mlle de Forant,

Your proposal cannot be accepted. The King means to carry out other arrangements for the foundation by your brother for the daughters of the officers of Île Royal.

— *Maurepas*
February 18, 1746

Guillot,

De la Mothe has taken the necessary measures for the preparation of the provisions and munitions that are to be put on board the vessel at St. Malo bound for Quebec.

— *Maurepas*
February 25, 1746

Beauharnois and Hocquart,

I did not wait for your representations to make provision for the needs of the colony. I purchased 80 pieces of ordnance of 4 calibre. Captain Sallaberry has left with 30 thousand pounds of powder, 350 firearms, and other weapons...La Déesse and La Société *will sail soon.*

— *Maurepas*
March 2, 1746

Beauharnois,

I intend for you to return to France and resume service in the Navy. You will hand over the general government of New France to the Sr. de la Jonquière, rear admiral. The King has judged it proper to recall you to France to serve there in the navy. The King is satisfied with your services, but [...] your age has not permitted you to take an active part in all the movements necessary for the defense of the colony. As M. de la Jonquière, who will replace you, is now serving under the Duc D'Enville, he will not take over the government until after the campaign. It is for this reason that I address to you the orders from the King as though there was going to be no change.

— Maurepas
March 15, 1746

Hocquart,

The King has granted you an extraordinary gratuity of 3,000 livres, which he will cause to be paid to your brother in Paris.

— Maurepas.
March 15, 1746

Hocquart,

The 24-pounders being defective, we will send 18-pounders for the armament of the [new ship].

— *Maurepas*
March 21, 1746

Memorandum from the King to serve as instructions for the Sr. de la Jonquière, Vice-Admiral, Governor and Lieutenant General of New France. Canada although suitable for solid and advantageous settlements, has made but little progress in the course of a rather long number of years. The first inhabitants were principally occupied in trading, drawn thereto by the independence they enjoyed in their operations. The success of those who have devoted themselves seriously to agriculture has served as an example, and for some years the colony has reached a condition offering opportunities to various enterprises profitable to itself and to general commerce, particularly as regards the fisheries and ship-building, which have enabled it to open up trade with the islands of South America and increase that which it had already done with the ports of the Kingdom. But this colony is still far from having reached the stage of development to which it can be carried. It is the intention to employ all practicable means to attain this end. Explanations relating to the public services, religion, administration, justice, etc., etc.[20]

Jonquière,

You are commissioned to serve under M. le Duc D'Enville as Vice Admiral. If the duke reaches Canada, you are to continue your duties with the squadron, and not cause yourself to be recognized as Governor General until after the operations on hand; during which period M. de Beauharnois will remain in charge of the civil government. In the contrary case, you will follow the duke D'Enville in the enterprises he would have attempted, after which you will proceed to Canada to take possession of the Government. Attached are instructions on the course you should follow to place yourself in a position to properly perform the duties as Governor.

— Maurepas
April 1, 1746

Duc D'Enville,

The King is much annoyed at the delays that have occurred in the departure of his squadron, for he feels they may occasion many obstacles to the execution of the orders that he has given you. It is too late to undertake anything, especially against Louisbourg. Besides the succor that the garrison has been able to receive from New England and even from England, Admiral Townsend will have had time to reach the place. In spite of all, the English forces will be held mostly to cover Louisbourg, and you will still have the superiority on the sea. The greatest obstacle will be the season. All the same, we still think you will have the necessary time to bring to a good conclusion an enterprise on Acadia. Instructions on what you will do in case you do take possession of Acadia follow...

— *Maurepas*
June 17, 1746

Bigot,

I approve your proposition for the keeping of the accounts of the squadron. I much regret the bad state of your health and exhort you to take care of it.

— *Maurepas*
December 27, 1746

Voila u
Couronement du derrie
qui a été desiné bien a
...

N° 378
POLYGRAPHIE 6 N° 37 B

ce voir ne la va bijours qu'alusee
qu cela

Chapter 30

Proof

Theorem 1. *Something remarkable happened on Oak Island.*

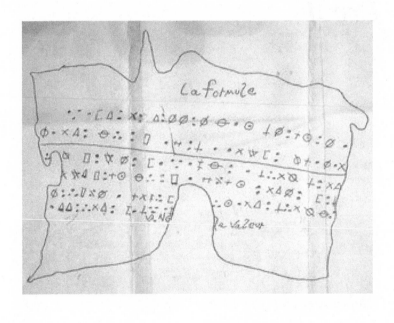

La formule

La valeur

Proposition 1. *The ciphers are real.*

The Mathematician began investigating the Oak Island story by obtaining copies of the two ciphers. The shorter cipher was the so-called 90-foot stone. The longer cipher, found in Zena Halpern's papers, along with two maps, had French annotations. Not knowing any French, the Mathematician downloaded a digital list of words into his operating system. /usr/share/dict/french contains 139719 words. He would have preferred a digitized version of a much older dictionary but was willing to assume that words haven't changed so much that it would hinder his decryption.

The Mathematician would make extensive use of a dictionary from the mid 18th century that had been posted online: Samuel Johnson's 1755 "A Dictionary of the English language."[32] The Mathematician also made use of an old French to English dictionary that he can no longer find, but has no current use for. He would also make heavy use of the translation features of his favorite search engine and browser plugins.

The Mathematician parsed the characters in the cipher into symbols and did frequency counts. There was ambiguity in some of the parsing, which added a slight complexity, and some of the characters were clearly cut-away for reasons the Mathematician didn't yet understand. The frequency counts suggested that the cipher was a simple substitution cipher, which was not at all surprising. More difficult ciphers were in use but uncommon. The Mathematician would have expected a more difficult cipher to be less artistic and use a more natural set of symbols, such as numbers, instead of runes.

The cipher using spacing for words greatly simplified

the decoding. The Mathematician began writing software to automate the decryption process, but in the course of parsing the symbols, and simply assuming the underlying text was French, the Mathematician quickly decrypted the text by just "grepping" through the French word list using regular expressions for the unknown characters.

The most challenging part of the cipher was along the boundary where the paper was purposely cut away, clearly removing some of the writing. In each instance of a word appearing on the perimeter, the Mathematician assumed an increasing, additional number of characters starting at zero and looked for all possible words. In most cases, only one word worked. In a few instances, the context of the adjacent words was used.

Very quickly, the Mathematician recovered the alphabet and found it consistent with the alphabet used in the simple cipher appearing on the 90-foot stone! The two ciphers read "forty feet below two million pounds are buried" and "halte ne terrer pas creuser a (qua)rante pied avec a angle quaran(te) (c)inq degre la hampe a cinq cent (vi)ngtdeus pied a vous entre le (cor)reidor a unmil(le) (so)isante (&) cinq pi(ed) atteinte la cham(bre).

The Mathematician noted that the 90-foot stone had a mistake (two f's, the second one being crossed out) so it was possible that the longer cipher also had some mistakes, some realized and some unintentional. Errors in handwritten cipher would be even more common than in plain text since it's hard to check the result. An accidental repetition of characters was easy to spot in a substitution cipher.

In the Mathematician's translation, two of the words appeared to have no meaning unless you replace an x for an

s. This is a common type of substitution when rare letters like x's and z's haven't been given a symbol. It could have also been a spelling mistake; the Mathematician is poor at spelling and good spelling skills back then seemed even less common.

As a digression, the Mathematician found the old dictionaries to be very incomplete; many of the definitions used words which had no entries! The Mathematician recognizes that it would be tedious to compile good dictionaries without computers.

The Mathematician tried to translate the text using the online dictionaries he obtained. He could get the gist of the statements, but the sentences didn't flow correctly. He turned to his trusted search engine which provided a much better translation: "Halte ne terrer pas creuser a quarante pied avec a angle quarante cinq degre la hampe a cinq cent vingt deux pied a vous entre le correidor a unmille soixante & cinq pied atteinte la chambre" became "Stop not dig digging at forty feet with an angle of forty-five degree the shaft at five hundred and twenty-two foot to you between the correidor has a thousand sixty-five feet reached the room." The online translator indicated that it clearly wasn't happy with the input and this could have been due to the age of the text.

The Mathematician makes a few corrections in the translations of the words that seem to be mistranslated. He next assumes that the author of the cipher would have, as he would have, abbreviated for convenience since writing cipher is also a long and tedious process. The Mathematician concluded that the decryption should probably have the following interpretation: "Do not dig in the earth past forty feet! With an angle of forty-five degrees is the shaft at five hundred and twenty-two feet. You enter the corridor which has a thousand, sixty-five feet to reach the chamber." Correidor for corridor appears to be a simple spelling mistake. The Mathematician doesn't understand exactly what this means, but the plain text appears to contain helpful instructions. At this point the Mathematician still considers both ciphers and captain's log to be hoaxes, but they are most definitely legitimately related ciphers, containing real plain text relevant to supposed buried treasure.

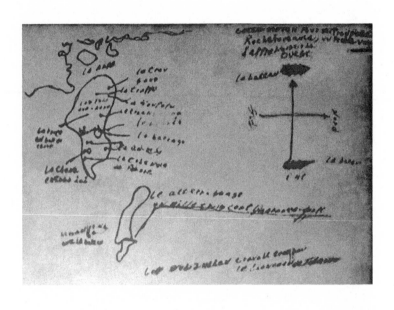

Proposition 2. *The maps and angels are real.*

The Mathematician, hoping to reach a contradiction, now assumes that the short and long ciphers are legitimate and authentic works of the concealers. If the ciphers are real, then the accompanying maps, if we take Zena at her word that they came together, might also be legitimate. The Mathematician, using screenshots and translucent "gimp" layers, overlays Zena's zoomed in map of Oak Island with the online satellite imagery of Oak Island. They roughly match to an accuracy much better than the Mathematician expected for a hoax.

The Mathematician then turns his attention to parts of the map he can't explain. In particular, the Mathematician doesn't understand the label "the angels" above the island.

Around the same time, the Mathematician reviews the captain's log that Oak Island researcher and Lagina contributor, Doug Crowell, found claiming to be involved with treasure and burial on Oak Island. The Mathematician follows the description of the journey from Chebucto (modern-day Halifax) to the supposed site of the burial. The Mathematician views the voyage using the online satellite imagery and finds the description to match perfectly with references to rocky islands, bays, and forested islands. This would be hard to do by someone who doesn't have access to this imagery or hasn't actually made this voyage.

In matching the surrounding islands, the Mathematician realizes that one of "the angels" in Zena's zoomed-in map matches an island above Oak Island. The other "angel" matches a now submerged gravel ledge that the Mathematician can clearly see through the water on the satellite imagery! This would have been very hard for someone to reproduce without satellite imagery and knowledge of the changing water levels over time.

This gave huge credibility to the map being authentic and old. The Mathematician, not knowing much oceanography, researched a little and extrapolated that it was easily possible for the water level to have been a few feet lower hundreds of years ago and that the water *pour*ing over the *angelic* ledge would have produced erosion. This detail is very encouraging and is not one that the Mathematician would expect in a modern hoax.

The Mathematician then tries to account for the other markings on the map. Notably, the other outlines of islands and hazards depicted in the map also appear in the satellite imagery. The Mathematician notes that the sizes of the islands indicate a lower water level at the time the map was constructed also giving more authenticity to its age. The placement of the triangular surveying stones also seems to match the historical record.

The Mathematician turns his attention back to understanding the cipher. The purpose of the two ciphers seems to be legitimately helping someone find the treasure. The Mathematician does a thought experiment. If he were on the island, and didn't know if he was on the right island, or not at the right spot on the island, what kind of information would he appreciate being left for him? The Mathematician reads about the markings on the boulders of Oak Island that were blown up by early searchers. These boulders would be something that anyone visiting the island would stumble upon.

Lemma 1. *The H+⊙ stone is a cipher.*

The unusual shapes of the cutouts surrounding the longer cipher now begin to intrigue the Mathematician. Did the cutouts align with features on the boulders? The only remaining picture of the markings on the boulders is referred to as the H+⊙ stone. There was thought that the cross in the carving might be a Knights Templar cross. The Mathematician can find no real Oak Island connection with the Knights Templar.[1]

The Mathematician assumes that these carvings were simply more cipher in the same alphabet, helping the treasure-seekers find their way. Zooming in on the picture of the H+⊙ stone reveals that the cross is not a Knights Templar cross but cipher that has run together. The H+⊙ stone's cipher is really '⯔ : + : ⊙". The H is actually the symbol for v which is similar to two half plus signs with angles. The two plus signs in this instance, have inadvertently run together, as can be seen, after zooming in, by the angles changing between them. This fragment of a cipher translates to "veues" using the same alphabet as the other ciphers. The Mathematician is encouraged that this looks like French plain text and ties the other ciphers together. This is a very important finding since the provenance of Zena's cipher and the 90-foot stone, additionally having been apparently lost to history, are in question. The provenance of the H+⊙ stone seems well documented.

Unfortunately, this spelling of "views" seems to be archaic but the Mathematician eventually finds it in an 18th century French dictionary and in a significant book of the 16-18th century with the title, "Plusieurs choses qu'il n'avoit

---

[1] the old lead cross is probably not as old as suspected

veuës", Antoine Du Pinet's French translation of Pliny the Elder. This book was very popular throughout this time period and actually talked about mining methods which the Mathematician found interesting but coincidental. This finding was also encouraging because a modern hoax wouldn't have likely used this spelling of views.

The Mathematician supposes that the markings on the boulder, something about "views", was intended to point the treasure-seeker to the right corner of the island where the stone triangle would be found. The Mathematician assumes the strangely shaped cutout on the cipher somehow matched markings on the boulders, not unlike the map in the Goonies movie where cutouts are used to orient the search. The Mathematician also notes a line and angle drawn on the middle of the cipher that might have been a part of this orientation. The Mathematician wonders if this is the first recorded use of this technique?

Lemma 2. *The measurements and angles are $\mathbb{R}$eal.*

The two measurements, 522 ft and 1065 ft must be horizontal measurements because it is clear that those depths were unattainable. The Mathematician doesn't understand the 45 degree angle, and first assumes it has to do with an angle in the shaft, until the Mathematician realizes that the H+$\odot$ stone has only gotten the Mathematician, still in his thought experiment, to the stone triangle. A treasure-seeker would need to know how to get from the triangle to the site of the pit. The seeker would need a direction and a distance starting from a fixed orientation. This perspective could easily be missed since the location of the Money Pit, at least its general location, is now well known. This provides more encouragement since a hoax perpetrated after the discovery of the Money Pit would likely assume familiarity with the location of the Money Pit, but the original creators of the Money Pit would not assume this familiarity for a future searcher.

The Mathematician is well aware that angles and distances are meaningless without a fixed coordinate system. The stone triangle left on the island surely provided the missing coordinate system needed to orient the seeker. The Mathematician's research tells him that the stone triangle was a well-known technique used in surveying. The stone triangles also, like the boulders, not being preserved, makes it difficult to determine the accuracy of the measurement to the shaft that the Lagina brothers have recently determined to be the original Money Pit. The angle looks reasonable from the historical record.

The measurement of 522 ft matches the measurement the Mathematician takes using the satellite image and known references from the shore to the pit. The Mathematician then realizes that the 1065 ft measurement matches the length indicated by the map's location of the "vault in the base of the earth"! The end of this line on Zena Halpern's diagram of the Money Pit marks the actual spot of the treasure chamber! Not 130, 140, 150, etc., feet deep, down the shaft of the Money Pit, where so many searchers have so tragically given their life.

Corollary 1. *X does not mark the spot.*

The Mathematician overlays the property layout of Oak Island and realizes that the treasure chamber is under Samuel Ball's property! Samuel Ball was a former slave, cabbage farmer, and early Oak Island treasure-seeker and landowner. *Did Samuel Ball have access to Zena Halpern's maps?* The

Mathematician recalls having heard that the maps were associated with the original finders of the island and that Samuel Ball was temporarily listed as being one of the original Oak Island explorers, but his name was mysteriously removed later. *Did Samuel Ball find something and want to then distance himself from the treasure?*

Samuel Ball having found something and having bought up the adjacent property seems encouraging given the information about Ball coming into an unexplained amount of money. Not vast amounts of wealth, but clearly more than can be explained by his known activities. The Mathematician found this encouraging because it would explain the failed attempts of the early treasure-seekers and the Laginas while helping explain aspects of the Samuel Ball mystery.

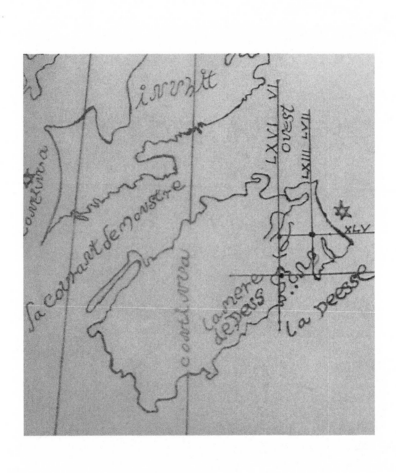

Proposition 3. *The boats and captains are real.*

The Mathematician now turns back to the three papers found by Zena Halpern and scrutinizes them for every detail. The Mathematician couldn't make much sense of the zoomed out map of the Acadia area; at least this was initially the case. The most prominent detail was the label of *La Deesse* at the location of Oak Island. The Mathematician, not understanding this reference, turns his focus back to the previous map. On the diagram of Oak Island, the Mathematician finds drawings of two boats. One indicated being larger than the other. One being a frigate and the other a schooner or snow (or so the Mathematician thinks, not being an expert in identifying poorly drawn boats or any boats for that matter). The one is labeled generically as "the ship," and the smaller one is labeled "the barque" which resembles a beak shaped boat. The Mathematician begins scouring the record around this time for frigates and schooners, but this doesn't narrow the search much. The Mathematician does discover what would turn out to be an important clue, that Jean Hiriard registered a schooner named LES DEUX ANGES, "the two angels", in 1750 for cabotage in this area.

Next, the Mathematician is intrigued by the orientation the zoomed-in map is drawn with. Most maps are oriented with North to the top. The Mathematician believes this orientation is done for two reasons. One is related to the approach that the captain's log indicated; the original concealers drew the scene as they approached it. The other and more compelling reason was to purposefully display "the angels" representing halos above the island. To the Mathematician, this gave a little more credibility to the captain's log and gave a sense that "the angels" were an important reference to the concealers.

These halos will turn out to be a crucial clue, when the Mathematician finally relates the principal concealers to archival references of the "angels of the island of Newfoundland"! The mathematician, at this time in his life not knowing the difference between Newfoundland and Nova Scotia, is later troubled until he sees a map of the area after the Treaty of Utrecht in 1713-15 and before 1750. After this treaty, the area of Newfoundland and most of Nova Scotia might have all been considered one.[22, 106] Additionally, the mistake might be the same geographical error the Mathematician himself made. Lastly, it could be a reference to other "angels" the concealers were considering. Two islands shaped like halos above another island would give a noticeable landmark to the early sea-faring navigators. The Mathematician later finds geographical errors such as Lower St. Lawrence referring to the waters below Acadia. *Had a principal conspirator never been to Canada?*

The other features on the map continue to check out. "The anchors" could easily be from earlier or later visits when ship anchors were lost, either purposely cut away or lost by a quick exit. This seems to be a common occurrence in the Mathematician's research and related to the phrase "cutting anchors". The map references a "valve" which matches the captain's log indicating air tunnels. "The marsh" or swamp is a well-known feature of Oak Island. "The dam" was discovered by the Lagina brothers and suspected by previous searchers. The "stone triangle" was already mentioned. The map references a second triangle laid in December indicating that more survey work was done in December after the initial work. The Mathematician would later corroborate that timeline separately.

The oak tree was referenced too. All of the details being spot on, the Mathematician began scrutinizing the text. There was a cryptic signature at the bottom acknowledging the hard work of the southern Indians signed by the Lion cub of Talmont. This detail proved very difficult to corroborate, but the Mathematician was able to find three, Boucher and Sallaberry not being among them, possible concealers that essentially fit this description.

Initially, the only insight this signature provided was that the signer was somehow familiar with the North. North of this area was Port Royal and Quebec. The Mathematician assumed that the signer had something to do with those places, as opposed to, say, most of the people involved in Duc D'Anville's expedition, who probably had never been to the colonies before.

Next, the Mathematician noticed that the translation given of the upper right-hand text of the map by the Laginas and collaborators was wrong. The translation had been partially corrected on the show, but the Mathematician noticed that it was still incorrect. The text actually says "this design for M. François D... Rochefoucauld, a little to the west." It took significant amounts of time to parse the poor quality of the text through the Mathematician's screenshot of the episode. The Mathematician finally realized the writer makes interesting s shapes, the same interesting s shapes that Hiriard makes! The Mathematician totally discounts Zena's interpretation of the maps being from the 1500s and finds many flaws with that interpretation.

The map was clearly made when there was a Rochefoucauld a little to the East, which was in September of 1746 on Duc D'Anville's expedition. The September date matches the captain's log. Next, the Mathematician wonders why the text says "this design for M. François D..." At first, the Mathematician thinks that it is a mistake. Almost all of the dukes of La Rochefoucauld are named François going back many generations. Duc D'Anville's case was exceptional. Someone simply might not have gotten his first name right[2]. *Who would have guessed that the duke was a Jean-Baptiste when almost all of the dukes of La Rouchefoucauld were François's?* However, the Mathematician then noticed that the map had been cut on this corner, much like parts of the cipher. The "M. François D.." might have actually been a concealer that requested the map and had nothing to do with the next line of the text. Perhaps "M. François D..." was the ship's captain or another concealer?

The Mathematician then turned back to the cipher and scrutinized the text even more. There appeared to be a date and a name that was partially removed. The name appeared to be le Vazeur (note the same l in formule). The Mathematician couldn't find any reference to such a surname and assumed it had been copied wrong, intentionally misspelled, or spelled phonetically.

The Mathematician then started working on theories explaining what had happened. The most likely, given the new evidence, was a cache of munitions or food stores that were left for Duc D'Anville. The Mathematician had to explain why the items were deposited and never recovered. The Mathematician assumed that something of value would have been recovered and found it very unlikely that the hole

---

[2]The Mathematician may even be spelling the last name wrong. The Mathematician equally sees it spelled Duc D'Enville and hasn't had the time to research the actual spelling

would have been refilled after the contents were removed. Backfilling would seem, to our environmentally unfriendly forebearers, like an incredibly significant waste of effort. If the items had a shelf life or were deemed no longer useful, then this explanation would work. However, the extensive excavations for something not very valuable or of fleeting value didn't make sense.

This stumped the Mathematician for awhile. Then the Mathematician noted in the captain's log that the original intention of the concealers was to build an access tunnel from the shore. These access tunnels, which were later misidentified as traps by the early treasure-seekers, turned out to be failed ideas from the flooding they caused. Why would the concealers want access tunnels?

The Mathematician suddenly realized the obvious: that whatever was buried was meant to stay buried, but easy access was still desired. This fit with the weapons cache theory, but not with both the 90 foot stone and the captain's log that said it was treasure.

Proposition 4. *The treasure is real and not real.*

The Mathematician then assumed to the contrary that there really was treasure buried in the chamber and that easy access was desired and hoped to find a contradiction. The Mathematician scours records but finds no indication of treasure significant enough to warrant the effort on Oak Island in the recorded captures relating to Duc D'Anville's mission.

The Mathematician then wondered why one cipher was in English and one was in French. Initially, the Mathematician assumed one was misdirection. However, the 40-foot reference was in both ciphers and fit nicely together. The Mathematician then researched further and found that the 90 foot stone was only reported when the treasure-seeking company needed additional funding and could not authenticate it having come from 90 feet. The stone was really discovered at the top of the shaft, later deciphered, and then concealed when the treasure wasn't found at forty feet for fear of losing funding. The stone was only revealed when someone realized that they could say they found it at 90 feet and that the treasure was 40 feet below this, to help justify further excavation. The activities of the Laginas and the captain's log indicated that digging that far was hopeless.

The Mathematician then realized that similar stones were found at the top of the pit and became certain that the 90 foot stone was actually the zero foot stone and was a legitimate help to finding the treasure, matching the other cipher. The entrance to the corridor would be found 40 feet below the surface. This is slightly above the depth that the Money Pit would have filled to when the original concealers broke into the underground water supply, as experienced by the Laginas and other searchers. The original concealers wouldn't have wanted this work to go to waste and would stage their next excavations from the 40ft level of the shaft.

After failing to go deep, they went horizontal. The Mathematician assumes that the access tunnels from shore were given up for fear of flooding and the additional access was either by the air chambers or the "hatch above the hole". So if all the clues found were helpful, why was the zero foot stone written in English?

The Mathematician realizes, in the course of his research, the ambiguity between the translation of livres and pounds. Livres are more like shillings. They are approximately 1/23rd the value of a pound (a shilling was 1/20th a pound). The helper who left the clues wanted to indicate exactly what was buried! It was 2,000,000 pounds—British money—not 2,000,000 livres! The easiest way to avoid this confusion in the context of a cipher was to put the whole sentence in English!

This however, immediately presented a seemingly insurmountable issue. A crucial obstruction. The Mathematician was excited that he might have finally reached his contradiction. The Mathematician temporarily ignored this potential obstruction since everything else was falling into place.

The Mathematician went back to the Le Vazeur reference and realized the most likely spelling was Le Vasseur. The Mathematician then found many famous Le Vasseurs and pursued many leads that went nowhere. Finally, the Mathematician stumbled on the coat of arms of the branch of the Levasseur family that were master carpenters and saw the symbolism burying the treasure under an oak tree would represent![61]

The Mathematician looked in Duc D'Anvilles mission for ships that were around in early September. Unfortunately this turned up nothing useful. The Mathematician then found a reference of a Levasseur, a sculptor who had mystery and intrigue surrounding his whereabouts during this time. The Mathematician tracked him to the ship *Le Fort Louis* and the captain was M. François Drouilhet. This was a major breakthrough! A Le Vasseur who was part of the Duc D'Anville expedition! This could also be the M. François D... who the map was made for! Making a map for the ship's captain made a lot of sense! Alternatively, the Mathematician would later note that the D could be a cutoff B in which case, referred to François Bigot, one of the major conspirators who would have been in need of such a map.

The Mathematician researched this vessel and found that it had lots of mysterious activities. The Mathematician, thanks to the powerful crawling capabilities of his favorite search engine, first found an autobiography that told an amazing story about this ship. This autobiography turned out to be Maurepas's![5] Maurepas's autobiography, him "doth protesting too much" trying to re-frame what he thought was an important aspect of his life's work. Maurepas's story placed the ship in exactly the right area, at exactly the right time, full of intrigue! Maurepas, in fact, focuses more on the story of this ship than on the entire Duc D'Anville mission.

The Mathematician studied the Canadian Archives for weeks and started seeing patterns.[7, 41, 67] At first, the Mathematician contented himself using his favorite search engine to crawl through segments of important books using the free preview feature with craftily constructed queries to see more and more of the text.[5] He eventually, after convincing his wife, purchased a very expensive, yet exceptionally well written, book which details the anatomy of the disaster of the Duc D'Anville mission[75] and a much less expensive, but equally valuable, book on the pirate hunter Captain Kidd,[119] which gave crucial insights. The same author of the Duc D'Anville exposition wrote many of the key biographies that helped the Mathematician unravel the Oak Island mystery[76, 77, 78].

Then the Mathematician found another breakthrough. On Zena Halpern's zoomed out map of Acadia, there was a reference to a Goddess at the very location of the Money Pit. This would turn out to be another smoking gun! Other researchers believed this reference related to the nature of what was concealed, like a religious artifact, or completely discounted the map. The Mathematician, after a great deal of research, could now match *La Déesse* to the name of a ship which was present in this exact area, anchored precisely there, at the same time! The captain of this ship was Jean Hiriard!

On this map, there is also a star that references the Duc D'Anville rendezvous location. The Mathematician then read that *Le Fort Louis* along with other key conspirator ships, sank in unbelievable stories. In the crucial case of the treasure ship, only the captain miraculously survived. The Mathematician, now having learned the name of the sculptor and the captain of the two ships that were implicated by Zena's maps and the other clues, finally had the critical mass of data he needed to unravel the story completely. The Mathematician now believed that he was on the right track since only a couple very simple assumptions kept leading him to discover more and more corroboration.

The Mathematician traced through any reference to any

of the people now implicated and found more people that were clearly involved. All the references lead back to Maurepas. The Mathematician downloaded summaries of all of the archived letters between the concealers, sorted them by date, and a story started to unfold. The treasure seemed to be the King's and the events read like a heist. The Mathematician, in reading the events leading up to the Money Pit, uncovered a previous attempt at pulling off the same heist! The events after the successful heist read like a cover-up.

Then the Mathematician kept returning to the obstruction that he mentioned earlier. 46,000,000 livres or 2,000,000 pounds was an incredible amount of money. Billions of dollars today, maybe even a trillion dollars if properly invested. France didn't have this much money to hide and how would it possibly go unnoticed in the historical record?[81, 85] It would turn out that it didn't go unnoticed. Only the theft, and the Oak Island connection, went unnoticed.[38]

The Mathematician uncovers the fact that both plots were associated to Levasseur and the money. There is a consistent theme of 200 men in the archives, and 200 men are referenced in the captain's log. 200 pick axes, 200 short handle picks, etc. were mentioned in the mission's provisions.[75] The Mathematician very roughly calculated that 200 men would have just barely provided sufficient manpower in the amount of time estimated to construct the Money Pit and the chamber. The key was assuming that multiple entry points were made, and this is reflected in the captain's log. The problem was not the manpower but the number of usefully employed men at any given time. The captain's log addresses this and gives crucial insights into the operation, and the division of labor that the Mathematician knew was required to construct the shaft, chamber, and tunnels.

The Mathematician, suddenly and very painfully, realizes that *Le Fort Louis*'s sinking would provide the opportunity the concealers needed to keep their work secret. Sadly and tragically, the Money Pit could never become the enigma that it had without a massive cover-up. Reading years worth of Canadian Archive summaries, the Mathematician begins to see the entire plot unfold. He finds unexpected corroboration in the American Archives and massive amounts of cover-up in the French Archives—almost all reference to the conspirators having been removed.[8, 39]

Then the Mathematician has another breakthrough. He finally asked himself: "Why did the French have 2,000,000 pounds in British currency?" It was counterfeit! Why does the King need a master sculptor toiling away for years in secret? He was etching the design of King George II shillings, in reverse, on the steel, hammer and anvil, dies used to strike counterfeit coins! These dies would wear out after so many strikes and need to be redone. Levasseur would perfect the process, oversee the quality and fix the defects. Why would Levasseur be given transport in the treasure shipment? He was literally the Creator and Overseer. The Mathematician's research reveals that counterfeiting by nation states during wars was common, that counterfeiting was a very real concern[3], and that all the equipment and resources were available to carry out this operation. The master sculptor could make dies that could flawlessly reproduce British coins, and the King could provide the materials and the equipment needed (fly wheel presses, silver, lead, steel, etc.). The counterfeit coin would benefit the King while

---

[3]e.g., Isaac Newton was made warden of the Royal Mint just 50 years earlier to help combat counterfeiting[80] and Benjamin Franklin would popularize the slogan "To Counterfeit is DEATH"[58]

damaging the British economy!

The King was well aware of the counterfeiting operation but expected the shipment to reach the King's storehouses in the colonies and for the coin to be used for his benefit. His actions after the reported sinking of the treasure ship indicate that he suspected it had been stolen out from under him and he continued to investigate the incident for decades. During this time, the King resumed the counterfeiting operations, holding a continual threat over the Sculptor's head, and presumably sent the future coin to the colonies in smaller, less vulnerable shipments.

The Mathematician realizes that shillings would be the most convenient coin for counterfeiting and passing on due to their size, makeup and use in everyday transactions.[12, 28, 66, 87, 93] The Mathematician learns that the most likely process involved silver clad lead. Maybe even using as much as 5-10% silver for cladding. This much the King could afford. The cladding would be done in some manner sufficient to avoid detection and lead has a very similar density to silver, giving the coins the right look and feel.

The Mathematician, trying to find corroboration, discovers that lead and silver were being mined and shipped to France and new deposits had just been discovered in the years preceding the counterfeiting and could be associated to the mines and forges that Sabatier was helping oversee. During the war, the French regime took over and operated the forge in Canada, which presumably processed the ore into lead bars which were shipped to France. The Mathematician can find references to these shipments.

The Mathematician did more calculations and realized that laundering 2,000,000 pounds would take decades. The laundering process is actually detailed in historical, first-hand accounts. Goods would be bought in America, the West Indies, or British colonies in Canada and then sold back to French people, especially the King, often at a markup. The process would create massive inflation in both England and France, which was also well documented. *Oak Island Inflation.* King George II would die toward the end of 1760 and new coins would soon be made, quickly rendering the uncirculated, mint condition, coin buried on Oak Island as worthless. Well, except if you have the patience to melt the coin down and separate the silver cladding from the lead.

This could explain the lead ingots found on Samuel Ball's property. The Mathematician can imagine Samuel Ball discovering the treasure chamber, feeling like he hit an amazing jackpot of unlimited wealth, realizing the currency is no longer good, and melting it down only to discover it's mostly lead! The lead still having value, and especially the silver cladding once separated, could easily account for the wealth Samuel Ball found.

The Mathematician is not sure if Ball ever found the treasure chamber or just found caches of the coin that some of the crew of the 200 attempted to hide while working on the island, imagining that they would be able to one day return to the island for the loot they stashed, not knowing they were all about to die. There's also a chance that Ball tried to directly sell the coins to people that perceived them to have value, which is similar to some rumors surrounding his activities.

The Mathematician began looking for independent corroboration of the coin being counterfeit and believes he found it in the archives. Explicit orders were given that forbade the melting of the currency, especially by silverware makers who melted coin directly into silverware, during the transition to the gold standard. Also, upon Bigot's conviction and sentencing, he was forced to give up all his possessions. There is much-to-do in the archives with the King being anxious to recover Bigot's silverware! The King, being well educated in the sciences, was trying to determine if Bigot's silverware had the same composition of the counterfeit coin! Did the coin lie at the bottom of the ocean as Maurepas claimed or was it in the hands of Bigot and the other conspirators as the King suspected? Bigot might have even bragged to fellow conspirators that he had made the items commemorating the coin, like candlestick holders, etc.

The other conspirators arranged for a powerful noble to get access to the silverware, to inspect the pieces in privacy and was permitted to, also in privacy, select from them any he wanted before sending the silverware to the King. This seemed like a good idea until someone realized that this, upon discovery, would greatly upset the King and would clearly implicate the one who asked for the opportunity to remove the pieces.

The creative solution found by the conspirators was to allow several nobles access, the Mathematician recalls it being five nobles, each one permitted to remove any pieces of their choosing. The King couldn't accuse all five, some might not have even been party to the plan, and there would be plenty of opportunity at removing and destroying the pieces that contained the proportion of silver and lead that the counterfeiters were using and that the King was looking to find. Historians viewed this activity strangely, assuming that Bigot somehow had a very interesting set of silverware. Very interesting, indeed.

Proposition 5. *The elements are real.*

The Mathematician also noted that Ball's first wife's mysterious disappearance could be explained if she spent all of her time melting coins to separate silver from lead. This process, done using the methods available at the time, would be extremely deadly, especially over long periods of exposure. In a related thought, the Mathematician wondered if lead poisoning could have been responsible for the disaster that became of Duc D'Anville's fleet. The Mathematician concluded that scurvy could not explain the expedition's tragedy, based on the studies he read: the symptoms of scurvy taking four months for people that are coming from good diets. The soldiers also didn't respond to treatments that were known to help scurvy.[55, 69, 74, 75, 111]

The symptoms that plagued the Duc D'Anville's expedition were consistent with lead poisoning, and the conspirators had concurrent access to more than 300 tons of lead! A very well-known, effective, and easy poison to produce is sugar of lead, a poison with an unconventional, very pleasant, slightly sweet taste. All that is needed is lead, vinegar, heat, and time. The Mathematician watched a video on the internet which detailed how easy the sugar is to make. 573 pounds of the sugar, which could have been easily produced by the massive factories providing the food rations, would be sufficient to nearly kill everyone on the expedition. The 20 grams needed to nearly kill each person could easily be put in the 0.5 tons of rations per person.[65, 79, 86, 100]

This was initially mere speculation of the Mathematician, but the Mathematician uncovered more revelations that indicated it might even be quite probable. Certain ships not experiencing the problem at all and some experiencing it at different rates; Maurepas requesting the ships be supplied entirely separately at the various ports; Maurepas having been clearly implicated in previous poisoning plots; captured American colonial documents saying the British didn't need to raise a defense in response to the amazing force of the Duc D'Anville expedition, and calling off their efforts to mount militias, after hearing a plan of *La Société*, the same ship that Maurepas sent in advance of Duc D'Anville's mission; *La Société*'s plan of harming its own country; and the British immediately spreading rumors that Duc D'Anville had been poisoned after only knowing the reports from Maurepas; all of this made the Mathematician almost certain that the fleet had been poisoned.[2]

The most revealing affirmation was Maurepas response to Bigot concerning the expedition.

> François Bigot later claimed that after he reached Versailles, Maurepas consoled him with the following well-polished aphorism: "When the elements command, they are well able to reduce the glory of leaders, but they lessen neither their labours nor their merit."[75]

Knowing Maurepas's strong use of wit and hidden double meanings, the Mathematician suspects that Bigot and Maurepas both know Maurepas is not referring to the storms that the fleet encountered which didn't seem to affect *Le Fort Louis* and *La Renommée* and clearly were not the key contributor to the disaster. The elements referred to lead. Maurepas really sees the victims as serving a purpose of reducing the glory of the King, knowing their sacrifice should be memorialized.

It was clear that Maurepas had been assisting the British and American colonies, by revealing activities and covering up the surrender of the King's holdings. The Mathematician, at first, found it difficult to explain Maurepas's intentions but will conclude with this later.

Proposition 6. *The Captain Kidd and Free Mason connection to Oak Island is real.*

The Mathematician finally, in wrapping up his research, wondered how the mythos of Oak Island became centered around the Free Masons and Captain Kidd. He perceived the misreading of Zena's maps as creating the unsubstantiated Templar connection. But the Free Mason connection was undeniably real, present in the earliest of searchers, somehow coming to believe that French treasures, possibly crown jewels, were buried on Oak Island. The Captain Kidd connection predated all of the theories concerning Oak Island. Oak Island appeared on historical maps as Kidd's treasure island, with documented connections in storytelling. There are also the early Anson expeditions.

The solution to this was the Mathematician's ultimate breakthrough concerning Oak Island. The breakthrough that helped tie everything together. The Mathematician long suspected that Sr. Hiriard and Sabatier were the same person. Maurepas referred to them, in a manner the Mathematician perceived, as interchangeable. The Mathematician found their handwriting to improve similarly over time as Sabatier was being trained as a scribe. A key revelation is Hiriard sending a letter to Maurepas written in the style of a scribe after Sabatier received the training. The official letters, which the Mathematician became well familiar with, always had Monseigneur, in huge letters, always signed as your humble servant, extensions on each line to the margins, etc. Hiriard, the ship captain had no business knowing these skills.

Hiriard and Sabatier appear on the scene at the same time and were absent the same times and disappear from the record at the same time. Sabatier was given many leaves of absence, in which Paule and others would assume his duties, providing him with opportunities to sail.

The first part of this final breakthrough happened when the Mathematician first associated Captain Jean Hiriard with the Captain Jean Troplong (meaning Too long in French—which was a fitting fake surname since Hiriard had indeed been sailing much into his older years). The same ship was listed on departure as being commanded by Hiriard and upon arrival, was listed as Troplong. The Mathematician can trace the use of the surname Troplong to the earliest of time periods of Hiriard and Sabatier.

The Mathematician worked backward from Jean Hiriard Jr, Bigot's valet and coachmen, who was with Bigot, even in prison, and the mysterious knight, Reynier or Regnac, who accompanied Bigot and Bigot's sister in exile.[38, 84, 118] The Mathematician suspected Reynier was Boucher was Hiriard Jr. and went by many names and was married to Bigot's sister, who also went by many names (there appear to be at least two sisters, the younger one using more names). The Mathematician first co-located Reynier, Boucher, Bochet, etc. and the Regnac aliases by discovering that all of these places were adjacent in Bordeaux, in the surrounding area of Chateau Bonnet.[4, 13, 33] Adjacent to this were the names of other conspirators! The Mathematician finally realized that surnames often simply indicated the area you were from or currently residing. Exploring these avenues resulted in the Boucher and Hiriard association.

The Mathematician eventually tracked down the marriage document he was searching for that actually tied the Hiriards to Bigot's sister. The Mathematician found a trifecta of a document: Hiriard, Sabatier, and Bigot all in one letter in a very important document concerning the eye-witness account of the surrender of Île Royal. This document is interestingly signed by Paule Sabatier, evidenced by his flourish, but who apparently had never signed the Hiriard name before because he spells it in a way that reads Hinard. Bigot would have felt that the eyewitness account that the King was going to read would be better signed Hiriard, Sabatier and Bigot than Sabatier, Sabatier, and Bigot! The Mathematician spends more than a week learning their signatures and handwriting and traces their movements trying to separate the various captains and conspirators with fake names and multiple aliases.

Then the Mathematician discovers written evidence that spies were being employed using lots of names to gain multiple accesses in the colonial documents of New York. A confidential agent, one that has access to prisoners, as Sabatier would. Bigot's sister's husband used an exceptional number of names, commented by a historian who believed it was to distinguish himself from similar names that were competitors in the same field.[52] The Mathematician learns that Maurepas is actually known to have been running a secret intelligence agency during this time! This finally makes sense in explaining how the De Goutins, Bigots, Ricouarts, and Sabatiers are one convoluted mess of relationships with multiple identities for the same person. The references to Bigot's sister and brother didn't make sense until these revelations.

Almost no record of Bigot can be found before 1739, even after people have dedicated extensive searches, which defies his background and future. All that can be found is a birth certificate which could have been manipulated. Maurepas, in his autobiography, makes note that Gradis's birth certificate contained a glaring error. Was this Maurepas's or his father's mistake? Or was this Maurepas's effort in reconciling other lies? The Mathematician discovers more and more about the Hiriards, Jr and Sr, the De Goutins, and Sabatiers.

The two Sabatier men seem to be together while their spouses, also De Goutins, stay in France. This seemed un-noteworthy until the Mathematician realizes that Sabatier being a cover story had no need for the late addition of a brother. His role would have been more naturally explained with a different surname. Why did they arrange for Paule, in his late arrival on the scene, to be a brother? What was the significance in the French-ification of Paul?

When the Mathematician researches Captain Kidd, the island in the fictional story does bear a striking resemblance to Oak Island and the Mathematician's current understandings of the inner workings of the treasure chamber. William Kidd, however, turned out to be a pathetic pirate and we now know definitively that he had nothing to do with Oak Island, except the notoriety which enabled the Oak Island story to linger.

The Mathematician sees the next part of this break-through happen when he reads the local Acadian lore of Oak Island that indicates that someone who sailed with William Kidd, an old pirate on his deathbed, revealed that he buried treasure on Oak Island. He was said to have sailed with lots of bars of gold, and he accurately described the Money Pit. An old pirate having previously sailed with Kidd but subsequently hiding treasure on Oak Island could easily be misinterpreted as the treasure being from one of William Kidd's expeditions.

Captain Kid's Farewel to the Seas, or the Famous Pirate's Lament.

To the Tune of, Coming Down.

MY Name is Captain Kid who has fail'd,&c. At famous Mallabar when we fail'd, &c,
My Name is Captain Kid,who has faild, At famous Mallabar when we fail'd,
My Name is Captain Kid, At famous Mallabar
what the Laws did still forbid, We went ashore each Tar,
Unluckily I did while I fail'd. And rob'd the Natives there when we fail'd.
Upon the Ocean wide, when I fail'd, &c. Then after this we chas'd while we fail'd &c,
Upon the Ocean wide, when I fail'd, &c, Then after this we chas'd while we fail'd,
upon the Ocean wide, Then after this we chas'd
I robb'd on e'ery fide, A Rich Armenian, grac'd, (fail'd
With most Ambitious Pride, when I fail'd, With Wealth which we embrac'd, while we
My Faults I will display while I fail'd. &c. Many Moorish Ships we took while we fail'd
My Faults I will display while I fail'd, &c, Many Moorish Ships we took while we fail'd
My Faults I will display, Many Moorish Ships we took,
Committed day by day We did still for plunder look,
Many long Leagues from shore. when I fail'd &c. All Conscience we forsook while we fail'd,
Many long Leagues from shore, when I fail'd I Captain Culliford while I faild, &c.
Many long Leagues from shore, I Captain Culliford while I fail'd
I murder'd William More, I Captain Culliford
And laid him in his gore, when I fail'd. Did many Merchants board,
Because a word he spoke when I fail'd &c. Which did much Wealth afford, while we fail'd
Because a word he spoke when I fail'd, Two hundred Bars of Gold, while we fail'd,
Because a word he spoke, Two hundred Bars of Gold while we fail'd,
I with a bucket broke, Two hundred Bars of Gold
His Scull at one sad stroke while I fail'd. And Rix Dollars manifold,
I strook with a good will when I fail'd, &c, We seized uncontroul'd while we faild.
I strook with a good will when I fail'd, St. John a Ship of Fame when we fail'd &c,
I strook with a good will, St. John a Ship of Fame when we fail'd
And did the Gunner Kill St. John a Ship of Fame,
As being cruel still when I fail'd. We plundered when she came
A Quida Merchant then while I fail'd, &c. With more that I could name when we fail'd
A Quida Merchant then while I fail'd; We taken was at last and must die. &c,
A Quida Merchant then, We taken was at last and must die,
I robbed of Hundreds ten, We taken were at last,
Affisted by my Men while I fail'd And into Prison cast
A Banker's Ship of France while I fail'd,&c. Now Sentence being past we must die.
A Banker's Ship of France while I fail'd; Tho we have reign'd a while we must die &c,
a Banker's Ship of France, Tho we have reign'd a while we must die
Before us did advance. Tho we have reign'd a while
I seized her by chance while I fail'd. While Fortune seem'd to smile,
Full fourteen Ships I see when I fail'd &c, Now on the British isle we must die,
Full fourteen Ships I see when I fail'd, Farewel the Ocean main, we must die &c,
Full fourteen Ships I see, Farewel the Ocean main we, must die,
Merchants of high degree, Farewel the Ocean main,
They were too hard for me, when I fail'd &c. The Coast of France or Spain
we steer'd from Sound to Sound while we fail'd We ne'er shall see again, we must die.
We steer'd from Sound to Sound wile we fail'd From Newgate now in Carts we must go, &c.
We steer'd from Sound to Sound, From Newgate now in Carts
A Moorish Ship we found, With sad and heavy hearts,
Her Men we stript and bound while we fail'd To have our due Deserts we must go.
Upon the Ocean Seas while we fail'd, &c, Some thousands they will flock when we die,
Upon the Ocean Seas while we fail'd, Some thousands they will flock when we die,
Upon the Ocean Seas, Some thousands they will flock
A warlike Portuguese, To Execution Duck
In short, did us displease while we fail'd. Where we must stand the shock, and must die.

FINIS

THE DYING WORDS OF
CAPTAIN ROBERT KIDD,

A noted *Pirate*, who was hanged at *Execution-Dock*, in England.

You Captains brave and bold, hear our cries, hear our cries,
  You captains brave and bold, hear our cries,
You captains brave and bold, though you seem uncon-
    troul'd,
  Don't for the fake of gold, lose your souls, lose your
    souls,
  Don't for the fake of gold, lose your souls.

My name was Robert Kidd, when I fail'd, when I fail'd,
  My name was Robert Kidd, when I fail'd,
My name was Robert Kidd, and God's laws I did forbid,
  And fo wickedly I did, when I fail'd.

My parents taught me well, when I fail'd, when I fail'd,
  My parents taught me well when I fail'd,
My parents taught me well to fhun the gates of hell,
  But 'gainft them I did rebel when I fail'd.

I curs'd my father dear, when I fail'd, when I fail'd,
  I curs'd my father dear, when I fail'd,
I curs'd my father dear, and her that did me bear,
  And fo wickedly did fwear, when I fail'd.

I made a folemn vow, when I fail'd, when I fail'd,
  I made a folemn vow when I fail'd,
I made a folemn vow, to God I would not bow,
  Nor myfelf one prayer allow, as I fail'd.

I'd a bible in my hand, when I fail'd, when I fail'd,
  I'd a bible in my hand when I fail'd,
I'd a bible in my hand, by my father's great command,
  But I funk it in the fand, when fail'd.

I murder'd William Moore, as I fail'd, as I fail'd,
  I murder'd William Moore as I fail'd,
I murder'd William Moore, and I left him in his gore,
  Not many leagues from fhore, as I fail'd.

And being cruel ftill, as I fail'd, as I fail'd,
  And being cruel ftill, as I fail'd,
And being cruel ftill, my gunner I did kill,
  And his precious blood did fpill, as I fail'd.

My mate took fick and died, as I fail'd, as I fail'd,
  My mate took fick and died as I fail'd,
My mate took fick and died, which me much terrified,
  When he call'd me to his bed-fide, as I fail'd.

And unto me did fay, fee me die, fee me die,
  And unto me did fay, fee me die;
And unto me did fay, take warning now I pray,
  There comes a reck'ning day, you muft die.

You cannot then withftand, when you die, when you die,
  You cannot then withftand, when you die;
You cannot then withftand, the judgments of God's hand
  But bound in iron bands, you muft lie.

I was fick and nigh to death, as I fail'd, as I fail'd,
  I was fick and nigh to death, as I fail'd,
I was fick and nigh to death, and vow'd at every breath,
  To walk in wifdom's ways, as I fail'd.

I thought I was undone, as I fail'd, as I fail'd,
  I thought I was undone, as I fail'd,
I thought I was undone, that my wicked glafs was run,
  But my health did foon return, as I fail'd.

My repentance lasted not, as I fail'd, as I fail'd,
  My repentance lasted not, as I fail'd,
My repentance lasted not, my vows I soon forgot,
  Damnation's my juft, lot as I fail'd.

I steer'd from sound to sound, as I fail'd, as I fail'd,
  I steer'd from sound to sound, as I fail'd,
I steer'd from sound to sound, and many ships I found,
  And most of them I burn'd, as I fail'd.

I spy'd three ships of France, as I fail'd, as I fail'd,
  I spy'd three ships of France, as I fail'd,
I spy'd three ships of France, to them I did advance,
  And I took them all by chance, as I fail'd.

I spy'd three ships of Spain, as I fail'd, as I fail'd,
  I spy'd three ships of Spain, as I fail'd;
I spy'd three ships of Spain, I fir'd on them amain,
  'Till most of their men were slain, as I fail'd.

I'd ninety bars of gold, as I fail'd, as I fail'd,
  I'd ninety bars of gold, as I fail'd,
I'd ninety bars of gold, and dollars manifold,
  With riches uncontroul'd, as I fail'd.

Then fourteen ships I see, as I fail'd, as I fail'd,
  Then fourteen ships, I see, as I fail'd,
Then fourteen ships I see, and all brave men they be,
  And they were too hard for me, as I fail'd.

Thus being o'ertaken at last, I must die, I must die,
  Thus being o'ertaken at last, I muft die,
Thus being o'ertaken at last, and into prison caft,
  And sentence being past, I must die.

Farewell to the raging main, for I must die, for I must
    die,
  Farewell to the raging main, for I must die;
Farewell to the raging main, to Turkey, France and Spain
  I shall ne'er see you again, for I must die.

To Newgate now I'm caft, and must die, and must die,
  To Newgate now I'm caft, and muft die;
To Newgate now I'm caft, with a sad heavy heart,
  To receive my juft desert, I must die.

To Execution-Dock, I must go, I must go,
  To Execution-Dock, I must go;
To Execution-Dock, will many thousand flock,
  But I must bare the shock, and must die.

Come all you young and old, see me die, see me die,
  Come all you young and old, see me die;
Come all you young and old, you're welcome to my gold,
  For by't I've lost my soul, and must die.

Take warning now by me, for I must die, for I must die,
  Take warning now by me, for I must die;
Take warning now by me, and shun bad company,
  Left you come to hell with me, for I must die.
  Left you come to hell with me, for I must die.

Proposition 7. *The dying words were real.*

The Mathematician started looking at the crew who sailed with William Kidd. The most obvious candidate was Robert Culliford, an excellent pirate, very much to the contrary of William Kidd. Culliford miraculously escaped Execution Dock at the same time Kidd and his shipmates were hanged.

The Mathematician learned that Culliford mysteriously disappeared right before Sabatier mysteriously appeared![45, 108, 119] The Mathematician then learned that Daniel Defoe had bargained for his release from the same prison in exchange for his services as a spy, that war between England and France had just started up again, and realized that Culliford would be an ideal spy.[91, 94]

History would record that Culliford was released in exchange for the testimony to convict someone that ended up being pardoned. This made no sense. Except that the pardoned person then served as a privateer for the pardoning nation.[110] Was Samuel Burges pardoned in exchange for his service? Did Culliford agree to a similar arrangement?

The Mathematician continually tries to relate Culliford to Sabatier and he finally has the most amazing breakthrough. The Mathematician finds "The dying words of Captain Robert Kidd, a noted pirate, who was hanged at Execution-Dock, in England."[82] A haunting, lamentful, "broadside" ballad put to music.[4] There are two versions known to exist. They both clearly come from revisions of an older document. The original version might, sadly, no longer exist. Historians

---

[4]The version "Captain Kidd by Waterson: Carthy on Fishes and Fine Yellow Sand. 2004, Topic Records" is particularly good, although sings William Kidd instead of Robert Kidd

believe there are lots of inaccuracies in the tales they convey and exploits that were larger than life compared to the recorded histories of these pirates.

The versions mishmash between the activities of William Kidd and Robert Culliford and seem to have been rearranged and modified for either propaganda or artistic purposes.

The versions clearly aren't written by William Kidd. William Kidd wouldn't write that he murdered William Moore. Kidd went to the grave claiming that it was not murder. Taking the two versions combined tells a story of how William Kidd was a horrible pirate and then lays out his faults and a very short list of minor accomplishments—most significantly breaking William Moore's skull with a bucket. The story then goes on to talk about Robert Culliford who accomplished very much as a pirate. This lament was clearly written by Robert Culliford, as also evidenced in the title of the long version.

The long version is clearly almost entirely about Culliford, although the Mathematician believes it is still not in its original form. Culliford had no opportunity to kill William Moore. He likely killed Ralph Stout not far out from shore compared to William Moore who was killed many leagues from shore. The Mathematician believes that these edits might have been done by someone attempting to fix perceived errors.[5]

The short version makes the Mathematician believe that most of the confusion resulted from editing errors of someone not realizing two distinct and separate stories were being told, that of William and Robert. At first, the hardest thing to reconcile is the claim from the long version that Culliford

---

[5]just as Waterson renamed the captain from Robert to William

died in London at Execution Dock as we have no record of that. Culliford mentions 200 Bars of Gold which could be a reference to the crew of 200 with gold trim bars on their uniforms? However, the other version uses 90, so this might be a literal reference to bars of gold that he was transporting on his final voyage. Or was the 200 changed to have fewer syllables to sound better in the song?

One interesting feature is the use of ligature—an artistic style of writing which uses long f's instead of s's. The lament changes the use of ligatures within the document, which contradicts the advice of practitioners that the Mathematician learns in his research on the use of ligature.[63, 113] The Mathematician, himself, would have used this mechanism to secretly encode more content into a message (the reader may not be aware of it, but the Mathematician has, in fact, used similar techniques to encode more content in this very document). If the earlier words are interpreted as having ligatures containing ambiguity, then interesting, albeit potentially incidental observations may be derived. "As he sailed" becomes "as he failed", which is fitting and illuminating. Also, and perhaps more important, is the phrase "do not for the sake for gold lose your soul" which could ambiguously read "do not for the fake of gold lose your soul".

Is the patriarch reaching out to warn the conspirators not to pursue counterfeiting French or higher denominations of British money, coin that is on the gold standard? Are these bars of gold intended to be used as gold cladding? The Mathematician learns that the word fake was surely being used by the criminal world, especially in London at this time, and finds an etymologist who assumes it was coming into the vernacular in the middle of the 18th century although the first printed reference is at least later than 1775. The Mathematician learns that criminal terminology was intentionally meant to be concealed for as long as possible.[54, 117]

The Mathematician finds the inconsistent ligatures interesting but has no means to validate these observations. It is likely Culliford would try to leak information in his dying words but would have to do it deceptively, or the message wouldn't be released by his captors. The Mathematician would have done this, being a prisoner about to be executed and wishing to relate what happened while at the same time giving a warning to other conspirators whose lives are now clearly in danger, since Maurepas had just hung the patriarch out to dry.

Culliford references the "Rix Dollars manifold they seized uncontrolled". Rix is both an abbreviation for riches and common silver coin used for everyday spending: shillings, for instance. This could clearly relate to the Oak Island heist. Manifold is interesting because it possesses many interpretations according to 18th century dictionaries. Apart from meaning numerous, it also means in many forms, copied, or multiplied. This could clearly be a very real reference to the counterfeit silver coin! He then mentions "St. John", "a Ship of Fame", "when we sailed". St John was the French patron saint, Jean—the name that both Hiriard and Troplong sailed by! The Ship of Fame could reference *La Renommée* whose literal translation to English is "ship of fame". The Mathematician thought this could be significant but didn't understand the reference yet.

The long version of the lament has an interesting drawing of a lion cub looking across a pond at a swan. This could be the Lion cub of Talmont looking across the ocean at Paule Swan. Culliford mentions burying his Bible in the lament.

This could easily be the leather-bound book of parchment that was found in the Money Pit. There is a seemingly unrelated engraving of Captain Kidd which looks nothing like William Kidd but resembles Culliford and depicts him burying a bible. Other images of Captain Kidd depict him looking more like this engraving and much less like William Kidd.

It appeared, to the Mathematician, that when one combines the versions of the lament, that Culliford believes that William's greatest capture, was taking much of the notoriety Culliford deserved. Interestingly, some references only appear to serve the purpose of distinguishing the two captains. For instance, there is a reference to missing the ability to visit Turkey which seems specific to Culliford, the Mathematician finding no mention of William Kidd in Turkey but indeed finding that Culliford intended to sail there.

Lastly and most importantly, the lament also mentions Culliford seeing "14 ships", "which was too much for him", and "having been overtaken" he's "taken to Newgate to be hanged at execution dock". The Mathematician struggles to find any reference to this until everything, at once, comes together.

Sabatier was reported as unexpectedly and tragically dying on September 22, 1747, at Rochefort. This is the exact time period of a naval action preceding the second battle of Cape Finisterre,[35, 112] concerning a French ship having left Rochefort September 20, 1747. On September 22-23, the French ship "was sailing a hundred and fifty miles southwest of Ushant, an island off the coast of France, making its way to Santo Domingo. On board was the new governor of Santo Domingo, the eminent naval commander Huber de Brienne, Marquis de Conflans. There they encountered the 26-gun

British frigate, *Amazon*... The two frigates had a running battle with one another for hours. Eventually the *Amazon*, greatly damaged, ended her attacks after she caught fire. Four larger British warships then appeared distant and closed on [the French ship]. With badly damaged masts from the previous fight, she was still able to outrun them and made course changes during the night. At daybreak on the 24th, however, she was attacked by one that had followed her by moonlight, the Dover of 44-guns and commanded by Captain Washington Shirley. After three hours of battle, [the French ship] had two masts severely damaged and was sinking. The Marquis de Conflans had been wounded, and they had lost fifty men and most of their gun crew officers."[25]

Around this same time, a British squadron of 14 ships of the line had left Plymouth on August 20 and were sailing on a path that would take the 14 ships right into the melee on their way to Spain.

The captain of the French ship seeing these 14 ships of the line and seeing no other options, "was forced into lowering the flag and the frigate was taken over. Captain Shirley towed the ship to Plymouth where she was surveyed, repaired, and commissioned into the royal navy.... The same Captain Shirley became her first British commander in January of 1748."[25]

This French ship was *La Renommée*! The same ship that escorted the Oak Island Treasure! The ship mentioned in Culliford's lament. The Mathematician checked the sailing records of the time and was shocked to learn that the last recorded captain of *La Renommée* having just sailed from Quebec to La Rochelle was Jean Troplong![6] Which we know

---

[6]History would record several captains aboard *La Renommée*[24] in-

to be Jean Hiriard! Captain Washington Shirley was a Grand Master of the Masonic Temple![23] This explaining the early Masonic focus of the searchers! Captain Shirley also became captain of *La Renommée* after it was repaired. Did Shirley, Vice Admiral of the White, and George Anson, 1st Baron Anson, Admiral of the Fleet, interrogate Sabatier and take possession of the papers that Sabatier stowed aboard *La Renommée*, the papers that would become known as Zena Halpern's cipher, map, and diagram of the Money Pit? The dying old pirate who once sailed with, and under the same name as, Captain Kidd, attempting to save his life, revealing the Money Pit and later being killed, his body sent back to France sometime around November, or shortly thereafter, when Maurepas finally reported to Bigot that they were going to be able to send back Sabatier's body to his brother so that he could be laid to rest in Canada. The Masons, Admiral Anson, Sabatier, Hiriard, Culliford, Captain Kidd, Oak Island!

cluding Sabatier, Conflans, François Aleno de Saint-Alouarn

Part XI

Conclusion

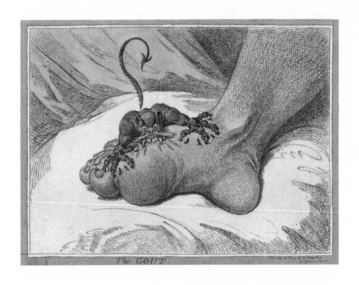

The GOUT

Chapter 31

What's in a Name?

Historians disagree on the origin of the words Bigot and Saboteur. There is no doubt that Bigot is a French creation of unknown origin. Bigot probably came from "By God" in the late 16th century and eventually taken to mean religious hypocrite.[88] François Bigot would embody and transcend the very meaning of the word: intolerant towards those of any difference. Bigot would leave 18th century France with a whole new understanding of the word.

There is also no doubt that Saboteur is a word of both French and English origins. The same is true of Sabatier. Historians have been completely baffled by this word.[109] There is no doubt, in the Mathematician's mind, that Saboteur came from Sabatier's actions in the forges of St. Maurice, the 3,400 guns procured by the militia that all turned out to be defective and/or never delivered, the arming of Duc D'Anville's ships with cannons that couldn't fire, the provisioning of the fleet with poisoned food, the absconding off with the King's military funding, and the subsequent fires in the lower forge and potash establishment.

Sabatier was the embodiment of the very word of Saboteur and a lesson in its danger and effectiveness. Sabatier's actions were known by top French and English military leaders involved in these operations. Many influential military leaders knew of Sabatier's activities at the time, and many more officials would discover them after the fact. Military leaders would doubtlessly use this example in their tradecraft, continuing into later centuries but kept secret and confidential within their ranks. The word would surely be passed through military channels and eventually leak out into the world. Just as Benedict Arnold would shortly become synonymous with traitor.

The name De Goutin also appears to be a construct of Jérôme. The family members spelling it in varying ways indicated that there wasn't a strong lineage. Family members spell the name with every conceivable variation: De Goutin, Degoutin, Degoutins, Desgoutin, Deville, Deville Degouin, Deville Degoutain, Deville Degoutin, De Ville De Goutin, Deville Des Goutins, Deville Des Gouttain, De Ville De Goutin Bellechasse, Deville Degoutin Villechasse.[1] Further, there is no earlier evidence of this name in the genealogical record (the closest being English variations).[6] Was this a play on words? Goutin would mean "relating to gout," and gout was known to be the "disease of the King."[97] Were the Goutins destined to become the King's disease?

What else is in a name? What was in Maurepas's name of *La Grande Société*? Maurepas had all the personal wealth one would want. Maurepas wanted more, but not for himself, but for a cause. Maurepas's ultimate plan was to establish a grand society; to gain the wealth, power and influence necessary for overthrowing the monarchy; to present a compelling narrative of the weak and ineffective rule of kings; to promote dissidence to the point of rebellion; and to place the absolute power in governance in the noble Parlement. *La Grande Société* was to be a republic!

The Grand Conspirator's plan was interrupted in 1749 when he was removed from power in a coup.[98] Starting with the surrender of the colonies, the disaster of the Duc D'Anville expedition, and the collapse of the economy through Oak Island Inflation, the wheels were in motion and already beginning to fall off the King's proverbial cart. Maurepas would resume power under Louis XVI and manage to re-institute the power of the Parlement. Maurepas would intervene on behalf of the American states and help pave the way to the French Revolution. The revolution that would literally decapitate the monarchy and lead to a global decline of absolute monarchies while replacing them with republics and liberal democracies.

The Lagina brothers were right. Something truly remarkable did happen on Oak Island. ■

Chapter 32

Epilogue

September 11, 2018

The Mathematician's youngest daughter comes running back into the bedroom. His thoughts are back into the present. He looks at the digital clock on his desktop. 8:52. He tries to steal a little more time; he types the current date. Yes, it's still the 11th. "Good, it's not that late." His thoughts turn back to his daughter. "Time for bed, let's go get you dressed in your pajamas."

"I'm not cold because I'm gonna sleep in my clothes," she informs him.

"Okay, let's get you to bed." He tries to steal a few more keystrokes and then his thoughts become her words. "Dad, would you like to go on a treasure hunt? What would you like to pretend to be? A pirate going to treasure? a monkey? a lion? a Giraffe? Right? Huh? dad? a pirate?" He moves his gaze from his monitor to her, and she begins to smile. He's already smiling. He thinks of Angélique, of the mathematician's hypothesis, and how the Captain would have changed his gaze from the sea to her. To the Mathematician, at this very moment, the identity of the two little angels is clear. His daughter and the Captain's daughter were both just a few years old. "Yes, a pirate," he says. "Then I'm going to draw the head of a pirate," she informs him and begins to draw on the back of some paper he can't identify at present. He spends a few moments trying to do so and concludes it doesn't matter. "That's a beautiful pirate!" he exclaims. "What's that?" he asks. "That's his hat," she says. They laugh. "Okay, let's go to bed." And they leave the room.

```
] 100  PRINT "HELLO WORLD"
] 200  GOTO 100
] RUN
HELLO WORLD
HELLO WORLD
HELLO WORLD
HELLO WORLD
HELLO WORLD
HELLO WORLD
HELLO WORLD
HELLO WORLD
HELLO WORLD
HELLO WORLD
HELLO WORLD
HELLO WORLD
HELLO WORLD
HELLO WORLD
HELLO WORLD
HELLO WORLD
HELLO WORLD
HELLO WORLD
HELLO WORLD
HELLO WORLD
HELLO WORLD
HELLO WORLD
HELLO WORLD
HELLO WORLD
HELLO WORLD
HELLO WORLD
HELLO WORLD
```

HELLO WORLD
HELLO WORLD
HELLO WORLD
HELLO WORLD
HELLO WORLD
HELLO WORLD
HELLO WORLD
HELLO WORLD
HELLO WORLD
HELLO WORLD
HELLO WORLD
HELLO WORLD
HELLO WORLD
HELLO WORLD
HELLO WORLD
HELLO WORLD
HELLO WORLD
HELLO WORLD
HELLO WORLD
HELLO WORLD
HELLO WORLD
HELLO WORLD
HELLO WORLD
HELLO WORLD
HELLO WORLD
HELLO WORLD
HELLO WORLD
HELLO WORLD
HELLO WORLD
HELLO WORLD
HELLO WORLD
HELLO WORLD

HELLO WORLD
HELLO WORLD
HELLO WORLD
HELLO WORLD
HELLO WORLD
HELLO WORLD
HELLO WORLD
HELLO WORLD
HELLO WORLD
HELLO WORLD
HELLO WORLD
HELLO WORLD
HELLO WORLD
HELLO WORLD
HELLO WORLD
HELLO WORLD
HELLO WORLD
HELLO WORLD
HELLO WORLD
HELLO WORLD
HELLO WORLD
HELLO WORLD
HELLO WORLD
HELLO WORLD
HELLO WORLD
HELLO WORLD
HELLO WORLD
HELLO WORLD
HELLO WORLD
HELLO WORLD
HELLO WORLD
HELLO WORLD
HELLO WORLD

CHAPTER 32. EPILOGUE

HELLO WORLD
HELLO WORLD
HELLO WORLD
HELLO WORLD
HELLO WORLD
HELLO WORLD
HELLO WORLD
HELLO WORLD
HELLO WORLD
HELLO WORLD
HELLO WORLD
HELLO WORLD
HELLO WORLD
HELLO WORLD
HELLO WORLD
HELLO WORLD
HELLO WORLD
HELLO WORLD
HELLO WORLD
HELLO WORLD
HELLO WORLD
HELLO WORLD
HELLO WORLD
HELLO WORLD
HELLO WORLD
HELLO WORLD
HELLO WORLD
HELLO WORLD
HELLO WORLD
HELLO WORLD
HELLO WORLD

HELLO WORLD
HELLO WORLD
HELLO WORLD
HELLO WORLD
HELLO WORLD
HELLO WORLD
HELLO WORLD
HELLO WORLD
HELLO WORLD
HELLO WORLD
HELLO WORLD
HELLO WORLD
HELLO WORLD
HELLO WORLD
HELLO WORLD
HELLO WORLD
HELLO WORLD
HELLO WORLD
HELLO WORLD
HELLO WORLD
HELLO WORLD
HELLO WORLD
HELLO WORLD
HELLO WORLD
HELLO WORLD
HELLO WORLD
HELLO WORLD
HELLO WORLD
HELLO WORLD
HELLO WORLD
HELLO WORLD
HELLO WORLD

CHAPTER 32. EPILOGUE

HELLO WORLD
HELLO WORLD
HELLO WORLD
HELLO WORLD
HELLO WORLD
HELLO WORLD
HELLO WORLD
HELLO WORLD
HELLO WORLD
HELLO WORLD
HELLO WORLD
HELLO WORLD
HELLO WORLD
HELLO WORLD
HELLO WORLD
HELLO WORLD
HELLO WORLD
HELLO WORLD
HELLO WORLD
HELLO WORLD
HELLO WORLD
HELLO WORLD
HELLO WORLD
HELLO WORLD
HELLO WORLD
HELLO WORLD
HELLO WORLD
HELLO WORLD
HELLO WORLD
HELLO WORLD
HELLO WORLD

HELLO WORLD
HELLO WORLD
HELLO WORLD
HELLO WORLD
HELLO WORLD
HELLO WORLD
HELLO WORLD
HELLO WORLD
HELLO WORLD
HELLO WORLD
HELLO WORLD
HELLO WORLD

Bibliography

[1] http://www.acadiansingray.com/Appendices-ATLAL-DE%20GOUTIN.htm. 80, 262

[2] http://www.naviresnouvellefrance.net/vaisseau1700 (translate.google.com). 171, 242

[3] http://translate.google.com. Miscellaneous translations. 31

[4] http://www.google.com/maps. Miscellaneous directions. 246

[5] http://www.google.com. Miscellaneous search results. 8, 233

[6] http://www.familysearch.org. Miscellaneous genealogy queries. 74, 262

[7] http://www.collectionscanada.gc.ca/lac-bac/search/arch. Miscellaneous archival queries (translate.google.com). 233

[8] http://www.archives-nationales.culture.gouv.fr/en/web/guest/salle-des-inventaires-virtuelle. Miscellaneous archival queries (translate.google.com). 236

[9] http://www.blupete.com/Hist/NovaScotiaBk1/Part5/Ch02.htm. 157

[10] "Pedigree Resource File," database, FamilySearch (http://familysearch.org/ark:/61903/2:2:S53F-3S2: accessed 24 October 2018), entry for Mathieu /de Goutin/; file (2:2:2:MM3M-J86), submitted 11 May 2011. 80

[11] http://www.familysearch.org/tree/pedigree/landscape/LKQ2-BYF. 80

[12] http://www.royalmint.com/our-coins/ranges/historic-coins/historic-coins/hisx152. 1, 71, 237

[13] http://eng.andrelurton.com/Our-Chateaux/Chateau-Bonnet. 49, 246

[14] http://www.patrimoine-religieux.com/en/our-churches/ursulines-chapel--parlor--museum. 29

[15] http://parkscanadahistory.com/series/mrs/317.pdf. p. 30 (24) p. 253 (64). 72, 73, 128

[16] http://www.acadiansingray.com/Acadians%20to%20LA-intro-2a.html?highlight=WyJXaWxsaWFtIEZyYW5jaXMgQmFydGxldHQiXQ==. 81

[17] http://www.familysearch.org/tree/pedigree/landscape/MVQN-WP9. 80

BIBLIOGRAPHY

[18] http://collectionscanada.gc.ca/pam_archives/index.php?fuseaction=
genitem.displayItem&rec_nbr=2477940&lang=eng&rec_nbr_list=2477940. 119

[19] http://collectionscanada.gc.ca/pam_archives/index.php?fuseaction=
genitem.displayItem&rec_nbr=2492543&lang=eng&rec_nbr_list=2492543. 127

[20] http://collectionscanada.gc.ca/pam_archives/index.php?fuseaction=
genitem.displayItem&rec_nbr=2514399&lang=eng&rec_nbr_list=3070822,
3040543, 2514868, 2514403, 2514499, 2514391, 2514400, 2514505, 2514393,
2514399. 202

[21] "England Births and Christenings, 1538-1975," database, FamilySearch (http://familysearch.org/
ark:/61903/1:1:JMTH-Z5Y: 11 February 2018, Robert Colliver, 18 Mar 1665); citing , index based upon
data collected by the Genealogical Society of Utah, Salt Lake City; FHL microfilm 916,895. 53

[22] http://en.wikipedia.org/wiki/Peace_of_Utrecht#/media/File:Nouvelle-
France_map-en.svg. 226

[23] http://larenommeeship.com. 257

[24] http://larenommeeship.com/saint-alouarn-1747. 256

[25] http://larenommeeship.com/captures. 256

[26] http://rmc.library.cornell.edu/FRENCHREV/maurepas/default.html. 71

[27] http://threedecks.org. Miscellaneous queries including of ships, people, captures, etc.

[28] http://www.coindatabase.com/coin_detail_libras.php?cdb=G120401. 237

[29] http://www.historic-uk.com/HistoryUK/HistoryofScotland/Captain-
William-Kidd. 71

[30] http://gallica.bnf.fr/ark:/12148/btv1b53016910d. 71

[31] http://lebloguedeguyperron.files.wordpress.com/2018/08/plan_de_
niganiche.jpg. 71

[32] A dictionary of the english language: A digital edition of the 1755 classic by samuel johnson. http:
//johnsonsdictionaryonline.com. Edited by Brandi Besalke. Last modified: June 14, 2017. 209

[33] Inventaire sommaire des archives départementales antérieures a 1790: Clergé séculier (nos. 921-3156),
1901. http://play.google.com/store/books/details?id=WTdKAQAAMAAJ&hl=en. p.
225 (translated by translate.google.com. 246

[34] Blaine Adams. *Dictionary of Canadian Biography.* http://www.biographi.ca/en/bio/le_
prevost_duquesnel_jean_baptiste_louis_3E.html. 129

[35] J. Allen. *Battles of the British Navy.* Number v. 1 in Battles of the British Navy. Henry G. Bohn, 1852. http:
//books.google.com/books?id=PVE2AAAAMAAJ. 255

[36] Jean Belisle. Un levasseur à rochefort. http://www.erudit.org/fr/revues/va/1984-v29-
n115-va1170294/54256ac.pdf, 1984. translate.google.com. 34, 71

[37] J. F. Bosher. *Dictionary of Canadian Biography.* http://www.biographi.ca/en/bio/laborde_
jean_4E.html. 126

[38] J. F. Bosher and J.-C. Dubé. *Dictionary of Canadian Biography.* http://www.biographi.ca/en/bio/ bigot_francois_1778_4E.html. 37, 39, 185, 187, 235, 246

[39] J.R. Brodhead, B. Fernow, E.B. O'Callaghan, and New York (State). Legislature. *Documents Relative to the Colonial History of the State of New-York.* Number v. 10 in Documents Relative to the Colonial History of the State of New-York. Weed, Parsons, printers, 1858. http://books.google.com/books?id=hm33ADvPyZMC. 158, 176, 236

[40] Kevin Burns. *The Curse of Oak Island.* Television Series, 2014-2018. Prometheus Entertainment for History Channel, produced in association with Oak Island Tours Inc. and Tell Tale International Inc. 107

[41] Public Archives Canada. *Canadian Archives.* 1885. http://books.google.com/books?id= UDcEAAAAIAAJ. 233

[42] Michel Cauchon and André Juneau. *Dictionary of Canadian Biography.* http://www.biographi.ca/ en/bio/levasseur_pierre_noel_3E.html. 29

[43] In Collaboration. *Dictionary of Canadian Biography.* http://www.biographi.ca/en/bio/ forant_isaac_louis_de_2E.html. 121, 123, 129

[44] Wikipedia contributors. Duc d'anville expedition — Wikipedia, the free encyclopedia. http: //en.wikipedia.org/w/index.php?title=Duc_d%27Anville_expedition&oldid= 827441546, 2018. [Online; accessed 24-October-2018]. 157

[45] T. A. Crowley. *Dictionary of Canadian Biography.* http://www.biographi.ca/en/bio/ sabatier_antoine_3E.html. 251

[46] T. A. Crowley and Bernard Pothier. *Dictionary of Canadian Biography.* http://www.biographi.ca/ en/bio/du_pont_duchambon_louis_4E.html. 128

[47] T. A. Crowley and Bernard Pothier. *Dictionary of Canadian Biography.* http://www.biographi.ca/ en/bio/du_pont_duvivier_francois_1705_76_4E.html. 128

[48] Céline Cyr and Michelle Guitard. *Dictionary of Canadian Biography.* http://www.biographi.ca/en/ bio/irumberry_de_salaberry_ignace_michel_louis_antoine_d_6E.html. [Online; accessed 24-October-2018]. 71

[49] Francois Alexandre Aubert de La Chesnaye-Desbois. Dictionnaire de la noblesse, contenant les généalogies, l'histoire & la chronologie des familles nobles de france, l'explication de leur armes, & l'état des grandes terres du royaume ...: On a joint à ce dictionnaire le tableau généalogique, historique, des maisons souveraines de l'europe, & une notice des familles étrangères, les plus anciennes, les plus nobles & les plus illustres ... http://play.google.com/store/books/details?id=EJ5YAAAAMAAJ&rdid=book-EJ5YAAAAMAAJ&rdot=1 p. 97-100. (translate.google.com). 74

[50] Société d'histoire de Bordeaux. *Revue historique de Bordeaux et du département de la Gironde.* Number v. 5-6. 1912. http://books.google.com/books?id=Z1xMAAAAMAAJ (translated by translate.google.com). 171

[51] Jean-Claude Dubé. *Dictionary of Canadian Biography.* http://www.biographi.ca/en/bio/ beauharnois_de_la_chaussaye_francois_de_3E.html. 119

[52] Jean-Claude Dupont. *Dictionary of Canadian Biography.* http://www.biographi.ca/en/bio/ baudry_jean_baptiste_3E.html. 247

[53] Michelle Guitard. *Dictionary of Canadian Biography.* http://www.biographi.ca/en/bio/ irumberry_de_salaberry_charles_michel_d_6E.html. 71

[54] Thu-Huong Ha. Fak news: You can probably thank 18th-century british thieves for the "fake" in "fake news". August 24, 2017. http://qz.com/1061375/what-does-fake-news-mean-the-etymology-of-the-word-fake. 254

BIBLIOGRAPHY

[55] Mark Harrison. Scurvy on sea and land: political economy and natural history, c. 1780–c. 1850. J Marit Res. 2013 May; 15(1): 7–25. Published online 2013 May 16. doi: [10.1080/21533369.2013.783167]. http://www.ncbi.nlm.nih.gov/pmc/articles/PMC4337985/. 241

[56] Donald J. Horton. *Dictionary of Canadian Biography*. http://www.biographi.ca/en/bio/hocquart_gilles_4E.html. 119

[57] Joceline Levasseur. The sons of the sculpture pierre-noël levasseur. http://www.levasseur.org/doc/dossiers/200506_Fils_Pierre-Noel_eng.pdf, 2008. 30, 31

[58] Eve M. Kahn. How franklin thwarted counterfeiters. Dec. 12, 2014. The New York Times. http://www.nytimes.com/2014/12/12/arts/design/how-franklin-thwarted-counterfeiters-.html. 236

[59] W. Kirby. *The Chien D'or: The Golden Dog; a Legend of Quebec*. Lovell, Adam, Wesson, 1877. http://books.google.com/books?id=CFoqAAAAYAAJ. 185

[60] Eric R. Krause. *Dictionary of Canadian Biography*. http://www.biographi.ca/en/bio/goutin_francois_marie_de_3E.html. 74

[61] Paul Levasseur. Coat of arms - history and meaning. http://www.levasseur.org/en/The_Association/Coat_of_arms, 1997-2018. 168, 232

[62] Peter (1993) MacLeod. Treason at quebec: British espionage in canada during the winter of 1759. Canadian Military History: Vol.2: Iss. 1, Article 4. Available at: http://scholars.wlu.ca/cmh/vol2/iss1/4. 38

[63] David Manthey.   18th century ligatures and fonts, 2001.   http://www.orbitals.com/self/ligature/ligature.pdf. 253

[64] Mary McD. Maude. Dicionary of canadian biography. http://www.biographi.ca/en/bio/espiet_de_pensens_jacques_d_2E.html. 128

[65] NileRed. Making sugar of lead. Published on Jun 28, 2017. http://www.youtube.com/watch?v=1OjLuJyMmUQ. 241

[66] Rictor Norton. The georgian underworld: 12. mother haycock & coining families. coiners & counterfeiters. http://rictornorton.co.uk/gu12.htm. 237

[67] Public Archives of Canada. *Canadian Archives*. Number v. 1. Maclean, Roger & Company, 1906. http://books.google.com/books?id=rMRJAQAAMAAJ. 233

[68] Royal Socitey of Canada. Mémoires et comptes rendus de la société royale du canada, 1903. http://play.google.com/store/books/details?id=PsOQAAAAMAAJ&hl=en. 75

[69] John Pemberton. Medical experiments carried out in sheffield on conscientious objectors to military service during the 1939-45 war. 1 March 2006. International Journal of Epidemiology, Volume 35, Issue 3, 1 June 2006, Pages 556-558, http://doi.org/10.1093/ije/dyl020. 241

[70] Bernard Pothier.   *Dictionary of Canadian Biography*.   http://www.biographi.ca/en/bio/morpain_pierre_3E.html. 145

[71] Bernard Pothier. *Dictionary of Canadian Biography*. http://www.biographi.ca/en/bio/du_pont_de_renon_michel_2E.html. 128

[72] Bernard Pothier. *Dictionary of Canadian Biography*. http://www.biographi.ca/en/bio/du_pont_duchambon_de_vergor_louis_4E.html. 128

BIBLIOGRAPHY

[73] Bernard Pothier. *Dictionary of Canadian Biography.* http://www.biographi.ca/en/bio/goutin_mathieu_de_2E.html. 80

[74] Catherine Price. The age of scurvy. 2017. http://www.sciencehistory.org/distillations/magazine/the-age-of-scurvy. 241

[75] J. Pritchard. *Anatomy of a Naval Disaster: The 1746 French Expedition to North America.* MQUP, 1995. http://books.google.com/books?id=xqY9PRghxssC. 146, 234, 235, 241, 242

[76] J. S. Pritchard. *Dictionary of Canadian Biography.* http://www.biographi.ca/en/bio/denys_de_vitre_theodose_matthieu_4E.html. 234

[77] James S. Pritchard. *Dictionary of Canadian Biography.* http://www.biographi.ca/en/bio/sallaberry_michel_de_3E.html. [Online; accessed 24-October-2018]. 25, 234

[78] James S. Pritchard. *Dictionary of Canadian Biography.* http://www.biographi.ca/en/bio/lemaitre_francois_3E.html. 234

[79] Jesse Rhodes. Sugar of lead: A deadly sweetener: Did ancient romans, pope clement ii or ludwig van beethoven overdose on a sweet salt of lead? smithsonian.com. February 7, 2012. http://www.smithsonianmag.com/arts-culture/sugar-of-lead-a-deadly-sweetener-89984487/. 241

[80] Ian Steadman. Isaac newton was the world's original counterfeiter cop: Here's the story of how the famous physicist played detective to capture his era's most notorious currency faker. Managing Editor @HowWeGetToNext / http://howwegettonext.com/ Mar 15, 2016. http://howwegettonext.com/isaac-newton-the-world-s-original-counterfeiter-cop-870d35c4b9bc. 236

[81] José Jurado Sánchez. Military expenditure, spending capacity and budget constraint in eighteenth-century spain and britain. Revista de Historia Económica. Journal of Iberian and Latin American Economic History. Año XXVII. Primavera 2008. No 1: 141-174. http://e-archivo.uc3m.es/bitstream/handle/10016/19643/RHE-2009-XXVII-Jurado.pdf. 235

[82] Isaiah Thomas. The dying words of capt. robert kidd: a noted pirate, who was hanged at execution dock, in england. Broadside Ballads Project, accessed October 24, 2018, http://www.americanantiquarian.org/thomasballads/items/show/98. 251

[83] F. J. Thorpe. *Dictionary of Canadian Biography.* http://www.biographi.ca/en/bio/boucher_pierre_jerome_3E.html. 185

[84] Denis Vaugeois. François bigot, son exil et sa mort, revue d'histoire de l'amérique française, vol. xxi, p. 731-748. http://www.erudit.org/en/journals/haf/1968-v21-n4-haf2065/302721ar.pdf. (translate.google.com). 185, 246

[85] François R. Velde. French public finance between 1683 and 1726. Federal Reserve Bank of Chicago. July 20, 2006. Paper prepared for the XIVth International Economic History Congress, Helsinki. session 112. http://www.helsinki.fi/iehc2006/papers3/Velde.pdf. 235

[86] Keith Veronese. The first artificial sweetener poisoned lots of romans. 1/20/12. http://io9.gizmodo.com/5877587/the-first-artificial-sweetener-poisoned-lots-of-romans. 241

[87] Jill Walshaw. Counterfeiting in 18th-century france: Political rhetoric and social realities. http://hdl.handle.net/2027/spo.0642292.0040.005. University of Victoria. Volume 40, 2012. 237

[88] Wikipedia. Bigotry — wikipedia, the free encyclopedia, 2018. [Online; accessed 25-October-2018]. 261

[89] Wikipedia contributors. Jérôme phélypeaux — Wikipedia, the free encyclopedia. http://en.wikipedia.org/w/index.php?title=J%C3%A9r%C3%B4me_Ph%C3%A9lypeaux&oldid=796601805, 2017. [Online; accessed 25-October-2018]. 49

BIBLIOGRAPHY

[90] Wikipedia contributors. André-hercule de fleury — Wikipedia, the free encyclopedia. http://en.wikipedia.org/w/index.php?title=Andr%C3%A9-Hercule_de_Fleury&oldid=865540193, 2018. [Online; accessed 25-October-2018]. 133

[91] Wikipedia contributors. Anglo-french wars — Wikipedia, the free encyclopedia. http://en.wikipedia.org/w/index.php?title=Anglo-French_Wars&oldid=865066869, 2018. [Online; accessed 25-October-2018]. 251

[92] Wikipedia contributors. Bayonne — Wikipedia, the free encyclopedia. http://en.wikipedia.org/w/index.php?title=Bayonne&oldid=861880461, 2018. [Online; accessed 25-October-2018]. 81

[93] Wikipedia contributors. Counterfeit money — Wikipedia, the free encyclopedia. http://en.wikipedia.org/w/index.php?title=Counterfeit_money&oldid=863811898, 2018. [Online; accessed 25-October-2018]. 237

[94] Wikipedia contributors. Daniel defoe — Wikipedia, the free encyclopedia. http://en.wikipedia.org/w/index.php?title=Daniel_Defoe&oldid=864941158, 2018. [Online; accessed 25-October-2018]. 59, 251

[95] Wikipedia contributors. George ii of great britain — Wikipedia, the free encyclopedia. http://en.wikipedia.org/w/index.php?title=George_II_of_Great_Britain&oldid=865319924, 2018. [Online; accessed 25-October-2018]. 186

[96] Wikipedia contributors. The gold-bug — Wikipedia, the free encyclopedia. http://en.wikipedia.org/w/index.php?title=The_Gold-Bug&oldid=858834427, 2018. [Online; accessed 25-October-2018]. 59

[97] Wikipedia contributors. Gout — Wikipedia, the free encyclopedia. http://en.wikipedia.org/w/index.php?title=Gout&oldid=864131062, 2018. [Online; accessed 25-October-2018]. 262

[98] Wikipedia contributors. Jean-frédéric phélypeaux, count of maurepas — Wikipedia, the free encyclopedia. http://en.wikipedia.org/w/index.php?title=Jean-Fr%C3%A9d%C3%A9ric_Ph%C3%A9lypeaux,_Count_of_Maurepas&oldid=829051306, 2018. [Online; accessed 25-October-2018]. 49, 263

[99] Wikipedia contributors. John swann (pirate) — Wikipedia, the free encyclopedia. http://en.wikipedia.org/w/index.php?title=John_Swann_(pirate)&oldid=860607558, 2018. [Online; accessed 24-October-2018]. 63

[100] Wikipedia contributors. Lead(ii) acetate — Wikipedia, the free encyclopedia. http://en.wikipedia.org/w/index.php?title=Lead(II)_acetate&oldid=851646602, 2018. [Online; accessed 25-October-2018]. 241

[101] Wikipedia contributors. Louis xv of france — Wikipedia, the free encyclopedia. http://en.wikipedia.org/w/index.php?title=Louis_XV_of_France&oldid=864091225, 2018. [Online; accessed 25-October-2018]. 85

[102] Wikipedia contributors. Louise julie de mailly — Wikipedia, the free encyclopedia. http://en.wikipedia.org/w/index.php?title=Louise_Julie_de_Mailly&oldid=861193790, 2018. [Online; accessed 25-October-2018]. 146

[103] Wikipedia contributors. Marie anne de mailly — Wikipedia, the free encyclopedia. http://en.wikipedia.org/w/index.php?title=Marie_Anne_de_Mailly&oldid=852919735, 2018. [Online; accessed 25-October-2018]. 146

[104] Wikipedia contributors. Michel de sallaberry — Wikipedia, the free encyclopedia. http://en.wikipedia.org/w/index.php?title=Michel_de_Sallaberry&oldid=824193143, 2018. [Online; accessed 24-October-2018]. 25

BIBLIOGRAPHY

[105] Wikipedia contributors. Oak island mystery — Wikipedia, the free encyclopedia. http://en.wikipedia.org/w/index.php?title=Oak_Island_mystery&oldid=865484547, 2018. [Online; accessed 24-October-2018]. 108

[106] Wikipedia contributors. Peace of utrecht — Wikipedia, the free encyclopedia. http://en.wikipedia.org/w/index.php?title=Peace_of_Utrecht&oldid=865439041, 2018. [Online; accessed 25-October-2018]. 81, 226

[107] Wikipedia contributors. Pseudo-bonaventure — Wikipedia, the free encyclopedia. http://en.wikipedia.org/w/index.php?title=Pseudo-Bonaventure&oldid=851563390, 2018. [Online; accessed 25-October-2018]. 67

[108] Wikipedia contributors. Robert culliford — Wikipedia, the free encyclopedia. http://en.wikipedia.org/w/index.php?title=Robert_Culliford&oldid=857290656, 2018. [Online; accessed 24-October-2018]. 251

[109] Wikipedia contributors. Sabotage — Wikipedia, the free encyclopedia. http://en.wikipedia.org/w/index.php?title=Sabotage&oldid=865199200, 2018. [Online; accessed 25-October-2018]. 261

[110] Wikipedia contributors. Samuel burgess — Wikipedia, the free encyclopedia. http://en.wikipedia.org/w/index.php?title=Samuel_Burgess&oldid=854075293, 2018. [Online; accessed 25-October-2018]. 251

[111] Wikipedia contributors. Scurvy — Wikipedia, the free encyclopedia. http://en.wikipedia.org/w/index.php?title=Scurvy&oldid=865240294, 2018. [Online; accessed 25-October-2018]. 241

[112] Wikipedia contributors. Second battle of cape finisterre (1747) — Wikipedia, the free encyclopedia. http://en.wikipedia.org/w/index.php?title=Second_Battle_of_Cape_Finisterre_(1747)&oldid=837615682, 2018. [Online; accessed 24-October-2018]. 255

[113] Wikipedia contributors. Typographic ligature — Wikipedia, the free encyclopedia. http://en.wikipedia.org/w/index.php?title=Typographic_ligature&oldid=865052838, 2018. [Online; accessed 25-October-2018]. 253

[114] Wikipedia contributors. War of the austrian succession — Wikipedia, the free encyclopedia. http://en.wikipedia.org/w/index.php?title=War_of_the_Austrian_Succession&oldid=864694756, 2018. [Online; accessed 25-October-2018]. 85

[115] Wikipedia contributors. William f. friedman — Wikipedia, the free encyclopedia. http://en.wikipedia.org/w/index.php?title=William_F._Friedman&oldid=859209799, 2018. [Online; accessed 25-October-2018]. 59

[116] Wikipedia contributors. William kidd — Wikipedia, the free encyclopedia. http://en.wikipedia.org/w/index.php?title=William_Kidd&oldid=865525497, 2018. [Online; accessed 24-October-2018]. 55, 56

[117] Wiktionary. fake — wiktionary, the free dictionary. http://en.wiktionary.org/w/index.php?title=fake&oldid=50265402, 2018. [Online; accessed 25-October-2018]. 254

[118] Robert Derome with the collaboration of Nadine Grelet and Alexandre Lussier. Engravings in the history of french canadians. renaud of avène des méloizes (family) and chartier de lotbinière, pean, bigot, kirby. http://rd.uqam.ca/Sulte/RenaudDavenesMeloizes.html. (translate.google.com). 71, 74, 75, 76, 185, 246

[119] R. Zacks. The Pirate Hunter: The True Story of Captain Kidd. Hachette Books, 2003. http://books.google.com/books?id=TbqZAAAAQBAJ. 72, 234, 251

[120] Étienne Taillemite. Dictonary of canadian biography. http://www.biographi.ca/en/bio/la_rochefoucauld_de_roye_jean_baptiste_louis_frederic_de_3E.html. 157

[121] Étienne Taillemite. Dictionary of Canadian Biography. http://www.biographi.ca/en/bio/taffanel_de_la_jonquiere_jacques_pierre_de_3E.html. 185

66842944R00173